1-800-ONLY-FOR-LOVE

contemporary writs by

CHRIS BENT

www.chrisbent.com

Published in the USA by Chris Bent
Naples, Florida USA
http://ChrisBent.com

1-800-I-AM-UNHAPPY,
1-800-FOR-WOMEN-ONLY,
1-800-LAUGHING-OUT-LOUD,
1-800-OH-MY-GOODNESS,
1-800-FOR-SEALS-ONLY,
1-800-OH-MY-DONALD, and
1-800-FOR-VETERANS-ONLY
are trademarks owned by
Chris Bent and are used with his permission.

Also By Chris Bent

Available in Paperback and Electronic Versions
at Amazon and iBooks

1-800-I-AM-UNHAPPY
Volume 1

1-800-I-AM-UNHAPPY
Volume 2

1-800-FOR-WOMEN-ONLY

1-800-LAUGHING-OUT-LOUD

1-800-OH-MY-GOODNESS

1-800-FOR-SEALS-ONLY

1-800-OH-MY-DONALD

1-800-FOR-VETERANS-ONLY

Coming Soon:

1-800-OH-MY-BLACKNESS

DEDICATION

To Christina, Candice, Courtney and their journeys . . .

Prologue

This is meant to be a book for just one person. If just that one person is touched in some way to make their journey better, then the effort is not in vain. Each one of us can look back to one moment that changed our direction for the better. May this book, a collection of my writs and wit, find that pair of eyes.

Chris Bent

Kennebunkport
JULY 2016
www.ChrisBent.com

Contents

Chapters

Only For Love

This is the first chapter of 1-800-Only-For-Love. I was just moved to start writing again. Today, December 22nd was my father's day of birth in 1913.

 I never know where a chapter is going. I just start writing. Now. Not knowing the next word or sentence.

Funny coincidence. He being born 98 years ago today. And I start to write again, and about love....

Only for love. What we are capable of doing "only for love"?

Our parents are our first and most powerful contact with love. Unconditional love until conditions change.

From a very humble and conservative background my father built his successful life. I am now 4 years older than he was when he died. I had heart surgery, he didn't.

Do I now know more than he?? Do we know more?

Most parents really love their children, in spite of the difficulty as their lives aren't sorted out yet. The child will sense it and be altered. It's uniqueness being formed.

Give me more Love…

No love and you will never understand the full potential of life. For without love there is no life. Think about it. There is only emptiness and insecurity and evil.

Why is it that everything stops for love? Why is every human affected by love?… and wants love.

Love calls us to our highest state of being. Without love the hill is too steep. One will never reach their peak and be able to see everything from the purest of perspectives. Sitting down and looking down from the clouds….

Along the way the love of things and feelings must be dealt with. One will not have it easy if love is in all the wrong places.

What would you do "only for love"? How does this compare with what you would do for money? Or status… or image… or power?

At the center of every being is the call to love.

How that is answered is the ultimate defining of who you are.

How do you want to be remembered?

Give me more Love.

Reflections

All through life we reflect back on things that meant something and the mistakes made.

These images in our mind are part of the incredible uniqueness of each and every person.

Think about it.

No… reflect about it.

Reflect about reflections.

One of our first reflections is probably our mom looking into her mirror every day. We are small and don't know what a mirror is until mom or dad hoists us up for the first time to see our self. No way you remember it… but it did have an impact.

As we begin to age we are more and more drawn to the mirror to see what others see of us. Flaws are seen as an embarrassment not stamps of pride.

I can't imagine the hours in the lifetime of a woman in front of the mirror. 25,000? 50,000? Touching up. Adjusting the look. Mirror-driven to appear as attractive as possible.

Reflect about reflections.

Look at the giant industries created by the mirror. Fashion, clothing, cosmetics, even exercise… all promising to enhance how you look to another. Maybe with us guys, our car is a reflection of who we want to appear as… or our dirty T-shirt.

Reflect on it… LOL.

We live our lives trying to control how we look to others. Do we stop to ask them what they think? If it is just a description of how we look then we are just a surface reflection. A snapshot of our surface.

All day long we live in our minds. How can people see who we really are? We can tell them, if we have the courage… but most stay pretty private about who they really are.

Maybe what we love and how we use love is who we really are. It is not about the surface. It is about how we love others. Loving self is vain and cheapens all potential. But caring for others without thinking creates the reflection of a wonderful person. One you can be comfortable around. One you can trust and have fun with.

Your real reflection comes from how you manage your love. How your love makes the lives of others ever so slightly better.

I want to be known as "Do you know what he did for others?"

So the mirror to look at is really deep inside.

The faces you helped should be the reflection.

That is where your love potential is found.

That reflection will be remembered long after you are gone…

Puppy Love

Why is it so easy to love a puppy?

Why do we look at some couple and say it looks like puppy love?

We smile and feel good about any kind of puppy love.

That is lucky love. Doesn't get any better. Pure innocence.

The eyes tell you all. They smile. Oblivious to the world.

Or maybe as a young kid when we saw our first puppy. Instant comfort. Instant trust. The height of human love… so gentle and honest. Puppy love.

We want more of it. Look into the eyes of the teenager with his first girlfriend. They blush and yield to the overwhelming feeling of love. Holding hands. Kissing. The other person never out of their mind. We all can see it. Doesn't pure love just stand out? Our first addiction. But reflecting… this addiction is all about helping and caring for someone else. Protecting the innocence of the bond.

We close our eyes and see the one we love. We sleep and dream in clouds of love. We never stop looking for people to love. It gets

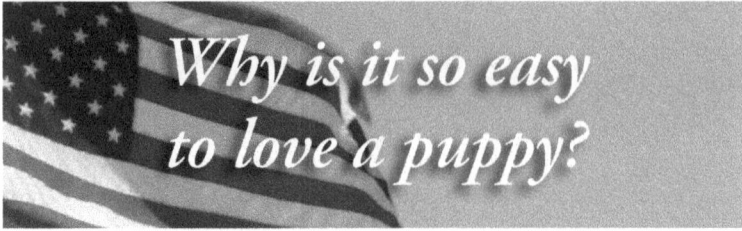

Why is it so easy to love a puppy?

harder and more complicated and more dangerous. Foolish things can be done if love becomes self-gratification. That is the dark side.

The love of power, or money, or things, is the antithesis of puppy love. People get hurt. All get hurt. It is the dead-end street. The sign reads "The bridge is down, road closed." No love here... and the individual looks back and realizes the time and years lost driving down the wrong highway. A personal tragedy dismissed by the arrogant and insecure.

Yes, puppy love is the best. Let yourself be a puppy again. Drop all your trappings and be alive in caring for others.

Use your puppy eyes to see the need.

Go over and take the hand of a needy person.

Puppy love.

Love Rose

Give her a dozen red roses.

Her face lights up.

There are some red flushing marks on her neck.

She blushes and her thank you is genuine.

They love getting roses. They need to feel cared about. They like being told they are loved. Roses do it.

Feeling love is special. Feeling unselfish love is wonderful. We all love it.

Love... Love makes the world go round and is the closest to truth we can get. And we all want to know the truth. Arms entwined, we wish for it to be forever. We don't want to let go. We don't want the sun to rise.

It would be nice to look at the world through the lens of a rose. Being picked and being given. With love for love.

And quite possibly a rosiness may appear on the cheek or neck. Blushing in momentary embarrassment of being touched way

Give her a dozen red roses.

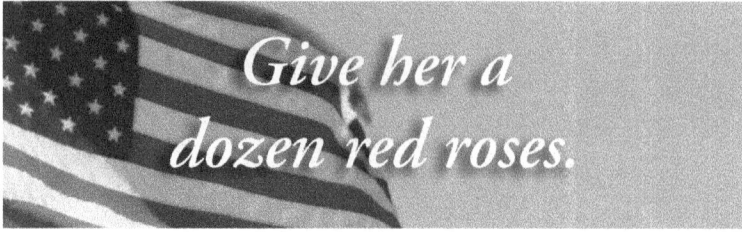

deep inside. Sometimes the red skin markings can almost look like a rose. Sometimes….?

"Send her roses" is often the solution when you are in "trouble"…

Let the roses do the talking before you dig a deeper hole… LOL.

I wonder if we can call florists "Love Merchants". Selling love for a profit? Or a Prophet…??? A dozen roses can cost up to $100 depending on how much you want to spend on her. You are counting on love to restore love. Love is precious and delicate and only survives in special soil and with lots of care.

Maybe there is a lesson for us in a rose?

Love is fragile and beautiful.

It can only be nourished in a complete yielding to Truth.

No one can lie or play with the Truth.

For love is lost at that very moment.

Love Laughs

What do love and laughter have in common?

Laughter is an audible expression of joy and momentary happiness.

You hear it.

Love overwhelms reason.

You see it and feel it.

Both can be faked… but there is a price.

Pure, spontaneous laughter is a path to the soul. The person laughing is baring his sense of humor for all to judge. It reveals as much as love… in a way…

The honest laugh is so easy to remember. It is a joy to be around. No matter what language the person speaks, laughter has no accent. Is not love the same??

Now you can pay money and go to an amusement park or Disneyland and hear mechanical clowns laugh, and laugh along with them. You can laugh at someone else's laughter. Or you can laugh at someone's fear on the roller coaster.

What do love and laughter have in common?

You can laugh at others as a sign of your approval or disapproval. You can laugh in judgement. Dishonest laughter can hurt. It can mock. It can cause pain.

Yet, the joke will be on the mocker in the end. No one escapes from dishonesty. The laughter faced will not be of his choosing...

Laughs of love communicate at the speed of sound. No thinking required. No planning required.

A glance of love communicates at the speed of light. It is so honest. That is the beauty of love. It is pure truth.

It is where everyone wants to be as much as possible.

In fact, life is just a pursuit of Love and Truth.

Truth and Love can be synonyms.

Isn't that funny?

Hold the laughter.

I love you.

Powerball Love

What in the world are they standing in line for?

The winner now gets over a billion dollars.

It is a dream of a happiness that only money can buy.

The winner will have a line of well-wishers 10 miles long for the rest of their life.

Friends that have always been in line to become your friend.

All of a sudden you feel their love.

Who can you trust?

How many times will you be asked to say "Thank you, but go away"?

Powerball love. Is it the love of power? Money brings you power... But we know money does not buy love. Or is it the love of love?... because everyone wants to be loved more? The smiles and the yesses are all so new after you win.

Win??? Privacy lost. Everyone wants to help you. Everyone wants to know everything about you, your family, your friends, and your history. That's Powerball love.

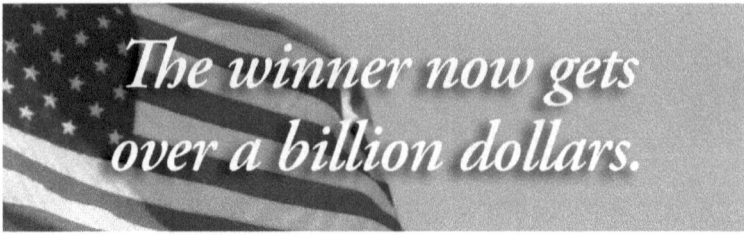

The winner now gets over a billion dollars.

Of course, when standing in line to buy a ticket you can dream about what you would do with the winnings. Who you could help by giving to others. What you need to keep for yourself. The first thing you would buy. Mortgage paid off. New cars. New house. Student loans. All bills.

Probably the best answer is to give it all away in smallish amounts to help as many as possible without changing their lives too much and keep a minimum for yourself. But keeping so little that they will know you no longer have any left to give away.

That your real richness came from blessing others with your generosity.

Nothing wrong with dying poor from generosity and compassion.

The only love in Powerball is being able to spread your love.

To share your blessing.

And to insure it becomes only a blessing rather than a windfall downfall.

Oh, by the way, there were 3 winning tickets.

Pray for them.

Love Is Powerless

Falling in love is the absolute best.

When that feeling first murmurs, you immediately and secretly direct your attention to it.

Glancing all around to insure nobody notices this feeling.... This weakness???

Then eyes lock for a second in recognition of possible powerlessness. The dance of attraction begins. Unsure. Probing for assurance. At this moment the momentum of love takes over and one becomes powerless... and loves the feeling. All decisions no longer in control. Total loss of self in compelling attraction. Been there??

You have to love something to commit to it. Hobby, sport, family, friend, work, worship. The more you can love the more you feel excited to be alive.

Those you love are under your protection. To love is to give up self. That is why in our selfish journey and our selfish world we are always looking for love. Life is about looking for love.

There are other loves. The love of truth. The love of values. The

Falling in love is the absolute best.

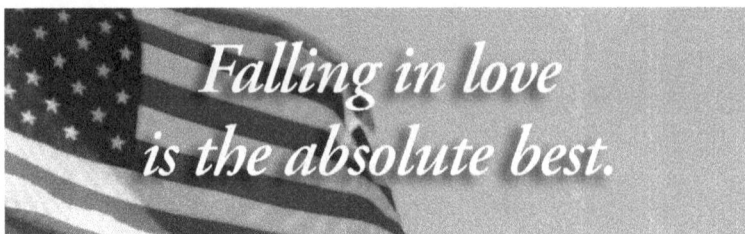

love of integrity. The love of wisdom. The love of education. The love of helping others.

This love is what makes the difference. This love is what makes one valuable. This love is what builds greatness… quietly….

But love can be misplaced. Love of material things can strip one of real character. Even love of appearance can get in the way.

When in love one feels a sense of truth. Love is so wonderful to feel. Truth is so wonderful to feel.

Maybe love is just a search for Truth. For the Truth does set you free.

True love needs to be found and protected.

I pray for the Truth.

So I can love more.

Broken Heart

Don't read this if you have had a broken heart.

Of course there are broken hearts and then there are Broken Hearts.

I guess a broken heart means a big disappointment. Something didn't happen that you had bet all your expectations on. Or worse, when someone was not telling the truth all along… Ouch, broken hearts really do hurt… and deep within your heart. Pain of an especially horrible sort that you don't want to talk about or share.

Someone told you that something was very true and it was not. Even worse, they were lying. Broken heart.

Broken hearts are to be avoided at all costs. And even worse is if you were the perpetrator. You will carry that burden and it will never go away. BHSD. Broken Heart Stress Disorder. Not funny.

A child dies. I don't want to be the mother.

Anyone dies suddenly. There is a broken heart.

You put your life into helping someone and you are not appreciated. Breaks your heart.

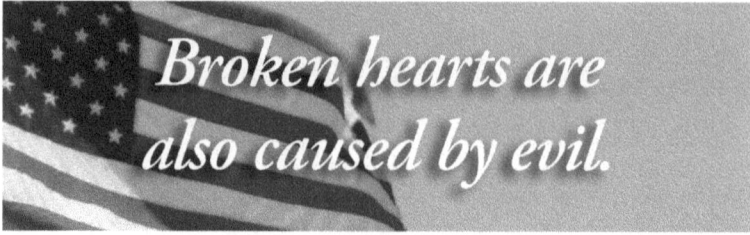

Broken hearts are also caused by evil.

There are infinite instances of broken hearts. "I don't love you anymore" is maybe the most prevalent. Really hurts. Takes time to get over, if you ever do....

Broken hearts are also caused by evil. Yes, evil. Evil in the form of selfishness or unfairness or bad luck. It takes a strong person to accept and move on. For some this becomes a forging process from which a stronger person emerges. Friends who stay close, console, and encourage eventually stitch the wounds and the promise of new life can be seen through the haze of tears spent.

Love heals all wounds... The right kind of love.

Given without strings.

There is a Saint for everyone.

Prayer helps.

All Is Fair

All is fair in love and war.

OK, so what does fair mean?

Who judges what is fair?

If you love your country and wish to protect it, then war it must be.

War isn't fair to all the collateral casualties.

Why is there war when there is so much love anyway?

We reflexively protect anything and anyone we love. We can't help it. If you don't protect love, then life has no meaning...

There are all kinds of love, be it cars, looks, money, or a person. What is it about that feeling that makes it so compelling? Is it an emotional sensation from the roots of our being? It can't be resisted, love...

I love success. But what is success? There is only one answer. That is in the helping of another person. That act is never forgotten. That act yields the greatest return. Helping someone.

You can run the fastest mile... you can make the most money...

All is fair in love and war.

But do these accomplishments stand the test of time? Or create the biggest smiles???

Is everything fair in love? No. Self-absorption is the danger of love. It can keep one from helping others. Be careful with what you love. Be careful with what is fair.

Same goes for war. A war on a disease, or poverty, or an evil is one thing. But in wars lives will be lost. I don't know how to solve it without more love.

More people helping more people.

More nations helping more nations.

More acts of kindness.

An infinite amount that will make fairness more real.

Love heals.

Everything is fair in love.

Nothing is fair in war.

Valentine 2

Be my valentine.

Show me your heart.

If at least on a card.

With pretty flowers, a red heart, and inside a poem asking you to be my love.

Or something mushy like that.

It works better on girls than guys.

They take the envelope and with maximum anticipation pull the card out. Almost afraid to look for fear it might not say "Love".

The "Thank you honey, dear, or John…" is felt all over the world. Anyway that is how she feels.

But it is not only cards that ask for love. There are masses of people who never get a card… who are living on the edge, in fear of what comes next.

Human contact from someone who cares and will look into their eyes with compassion and love. Food for the soul. Maybe just

Be my valentine.

smiles of thank you…. Maybe… On February 14….

Valentines of hope can be given every day of the year if we understand. Hearts can move from cards to random acts of caring all year long. The envelope is us. The card is the smile exchanged. Heart to heart for the brief moment… planting a seed of hope that pains can go away.

Encouragements of the smallest kind, given by any and every person, can unite strangers in a brief moment of honesty and gratitude.

Maybe if we take a magnifying glass to the heart on the card we can see the faint letters that spell "compassion".

Compassion is the key to love.

It is the prescription that will cure blindness.

It will make everyone a Valentine.

Lovestrong

I'm going to the gym to lift heavy love weights.

I want to be strong when love crosses my path.

I won't let it overwhelm me.

I will be in control.

I will have love wherever and whenever I choose.

I will be Lovestrong.

I will be able to look beauty straight in the eye and not blink or blush.

Except there is a flaw in this reasoning.

Love is the ultimate loose cannon. It cannot be controlled. It is the most powerful tool in existence when allowed to be pure. Not the love you pay for or arrange. That is not love. That is sensation. The wrong door, behind which is only pain and remorse.

To be strong in love is to relinquish control to your conscience, your heart.

> ## *I'm going to the gym to lift heavy love weights.*

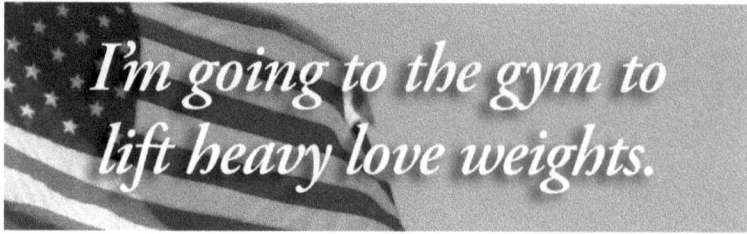

It will then lead you to where love is needed. And you will be amazed at the effect you can have. It can really be seductive if you let go. The compulsion to do more good will make you an addict to caring. You will be Lovestrong.

But to get strong you have to lift loveweights. Act after act of helping others, heavy love lifting, will give you the reassurance needed to help in even bigger ways. And it is not about money, it is about the time…the minutes and the hours you spend bringing your love to others. Smile and then move on to the next person.

Why that might even be the checkout gal at your supermarket….

There is much to learn to get Lovestrong.

It takes time.

It takes letting go of yourself.

Letting go of the mirror.

It will no longer be what you look like but what you do.

And you will be able to wink at God.

Luv

Yep, you guessed it.

It was so obvious.

How do you get to where you were meant to be?

There is only one way.

You have to get a Love Utility Vehicle.

You can't buy one anywhere.

There are no dealerships.

For that vehicle is you.

You can go anywhere with love, regardless how steep or painful the hill.

People will let you in if you are driving a LUV.

Where are LUVs made? I think the factory is wherever you are... alone and away from distraction. And capable of being seriously honest with yourself. No more lies. Just the Truth.

You have to get a Love Utility Vehicle.

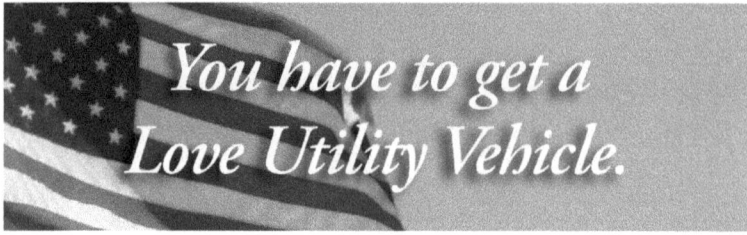

Think way back when you were honest, when it felt good to tell the truth. Where it felt good helping someone else. At the HOG, Helping Others Garage, you listen to others who have had bad journeys and how they finally got their LUV. Listen to how proud they are that they left their MUV abandoned out in the desert. Oh, MUV is Me Utility Vehicle.

How can you tell if your LUV is strong enough to handle the all the pain in the terrain ahead?

Well, you just have to start driving it and pull over as soon as you feel some pain. Drive closer until you know you are there. Find the eyes that are glancing with fear. Get out of your LUV and start the conversation. Find out what the pain is and address it with compassion and prayer. You will know exactly what you can do. You will have just planted a seed of hope with your love. As you walk away look back over your shoulder and catch the smile and wave.

When you come across other LUVs you can have wonderful conversations with their drivers. How they felt with this new exhilarating love. All they can talk about is the love given to others and not themselves. Sharing the good of love, not the aberrations.

LUVs Anonymous. LUVA.

Doing what has to be done.

Leaving no pain unturned.

I love my LUV.

Puppy Love 2

I got the call in church.

"Where is she? I cannot find Angel!!!!"

The collie was missing.

Primal fear in my wife's being.

I raced home. Stomach churning for her.

All was good. Angel was found by a neighbor.

We sat… emotionally exhausted.

Nothing like when a child, parent, or friend is lost though…. But a taste…

Puppy love is a term describing the love of a puppy and from a puppy. It is pure and innocent. When one is first stricken by love you can see the "puppy love" look on their faces.

What is it about love that is so infinite? More variations than stars in the universe. And more powerful. So much good to love. Most spend a lifetime searching for more love.

No puppy should go unheld.

Love that says "let me give to you". On pins and needles one waits for the answer. Maybe never given…. But when given the kiss is unstoppable. Get out of the way for the bonding of love. A new love unit is being formed that takes evil out of the equation.

Families that form in love, and age in love, have the ultimate protection. Don't mess with them for love can bite and love can fight. Hit my mom, kid, or spouse and you are doomed… so to speak.

It all begins with puppy love. Love that is still in its forming innocence. Should not everyone have a puppy? Those forgiving and yearning eyes that beg you to pet and then scratch behind the ears? Look again into her eyes and try to keep from melting.

No puppy should go unheld. No puppy eyes should not be looked into.

A puppy affirms the innocence and the power of love.

Take your puppy on your first date with anyone and watch them melt and look into your eyes.

Easy litmus test.

If they don't get it, then they don't know love.

Puppies are love magnets.

You can't lose.

All it takes is a little dog food and love.

Love You

"Love you" is the last thing said when you part.

It is so great when someone says they love you.

Even the worst of people yearn for a genuine "Love You".

Lives can be upside down… but they are still looking for love. Whatever that feeling is, it trumps all logic and problems.

If someone is in trouble, they need someone to love them. For love is hope and it calms the moment. Love makes the world go away… it makes the pain bearable. Everybody wants love. There is no life without love. No love and you are dead inside. You don't want anyone to know that nobody loves you.

But your mother loved you. Her imprint is in your need for love and what shape it takes. Insecure teenagers chase love like in a happy dance. Love for the moment is physical. Love for eternity lies in helping others find love.

If you love someone you want to help them.

When you fall in love with helping others you will finally love yourself. For the beauty of love lies in the smile of the receiver.

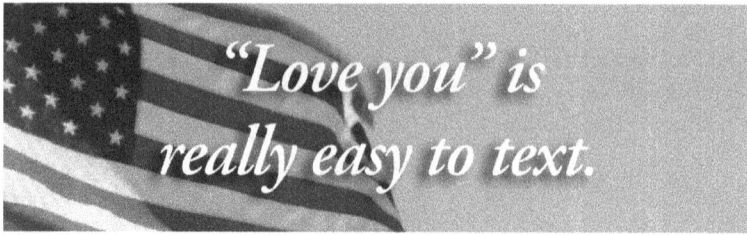

"Love you" is really easy to text.

You can show love by showing respect. You can show love by telling only the Truth. Love has a hard battle when it is so abused and distorted by media and gossip. They make fortunes off of feeding us "acted" love.

A hand that is held in love is one of the great moments in life. Where joy and peace bond in the privacy of shared feelings. Feelings that merge into an inner glow.

"Love you" is really easy to text.

Don't cheapen it by not meaning it or making it too casual. Love is the most important human experience available to mankind. When it is abused there is chaos and terrible pain...... and terrible tears.....

Love belongs to all.

Love cannot be legislated.

Love can only be given.

Takers end up miserable.

Isn't love Divine??

"Love you".

From A Distance

Ask a Veteran if he ever waited for mail call?

From WWII to Korea to Vietnam to the Middle East?

Hearing from home and kids and wife or girlfriend.

That letter was pure gold.

To be read often in the loneliest and most dangerous of places.

Because it was all about love….

Love travelling through space between the two lovers or family.

Wonder what it would look like from the space station if there were love lines rather than airplane routes? The number of love lanes is close to infinite.

The bond between those who love defies description. Once upon a time there were even love lanes from the moon.

From a distance everything can look fine.

Did you ever see someone from a distance who seemed happy but when close you could only see pain?

That is the challenge of love… to get close… to put your arms

around it… to share the pain… to kill it with love.

Little is ever accomplished from a distance……. Governments and bureaucracies keep trying though… wink, wink.

If we truly believe in love, then we have to get close. We have to feel the pain to understand it. Then by caring, reassurance, and love… mountains can be moved.

We all have a choice to make. Is it an offering in the basket at a church or the knock on the front door of the hurting? A smile and a "How can I help you?" starts the journey. Every time you love you feel good. Love beyond physical has a much greater return.

The Congressional Medal of Honor is given for extreme bravery. For risking one's life for another. This medal is symbolically available to you and me when we help someone who is dying inside.

To help is to love.

There is no time for self-gratification.

Doing what is right makes you a lover.

Need You Now

What is it about love that makes it so immediate?

Have you ever been overwhelmed by the "need you now" emotion?

Rushing to be together and the intensity of the first hug? And kiss??

We can be in dark places. A prisoner of circumstance cut off from all the world. Yet the "need you now" feeling brightens the moment. With love there is always hope.

You can't help praying for love. Because there are times that it is all you need.

Love is a universal truth. Love lives in truth. Love is the strongest force on earth if you let it be. It is our choice. Love is easily corrupted by selfishness and self.

When you are in love… don't we feel it in our hearts? That sensual flutter left center chest… LOL…

Love makes us protect those we love. It makes us able to reach out and help those who are hurting.

That sensual flutter left center chest...

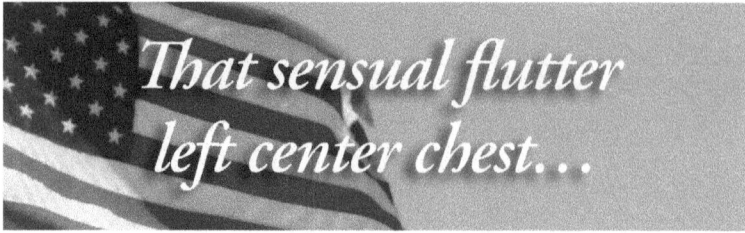

There are more people in our world that need our love than ever before.

Give in to love now…. Let it fill your being… You will be loved more than you ever imagined.

Think about how much all kinds of love from you can make a difference.

Just a little goes a long way.

Love is patient.

Love is kind.

Let love be you.

Just a thought.

Cars

Before cars what did men care about?

Cars take you to where you want to go and you get to drive.

Most of the time it is to something you love.

Or to meet with a person you love.

If something is important you go fast.

Or to prolong something you love you go slow.

We love our cars as they transport us to wherever want. And the thing we love the most is love.

Great paint job, lots of horsepower, shiny this and that. Love a car that is kept up.

Women don't love cars. They just use them.

Do women love men? Or do they just use them?? LOL.

Cars are really about destination. Where you want to go.

Think of yourself as a car… that only runs on love. High octane love.

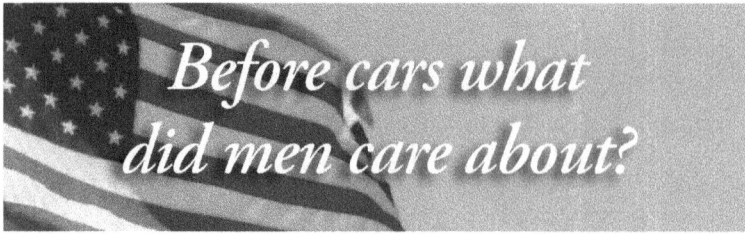

Before cars what did men care about?

Helping someone else is what love is really all about. To get there is more important than what you drive. To be able to make a difference is the greatest award. We are remembered by what we do for others. Not what car we drove.

Real pride is achieved from knowing you helped; that someone else's life is better because you got there on time and made a smile appear once again on the face you are saving.

So this really isn't about cars. Nor what you look like. It is really about trying to be a vehicle for values and love.

The truth must be spread everywhere.

And truth reveals itself only through love.

Honesty and Humility should sit in your back seat.

With you driving and Compassion in shotgun.

Guaranteed

Today everything must have a warranty.

Or guarantee that nothing will go wrong.

It gets fixed free of charge, no contest.

Get married and get a license and you supposedly have a guarantee that you will live happily ever after. Break the warranty and you are guaranteed a very uncomfortable settlement…

A car is easier to take care of. To keep running and looking shiny.

A man's handshake used to be a guarantee. His word meant something. No paperwork required. It worked. Of course you had to be able to size up the partner. And it is a good feeling to trust and be trustworthy.

Today nobody trusts anything. And the legal industry is surfing this giant wave at Mavericks?? 30 Foot face….. Like Wall Street….where you drive down to get money. And can trust everybody who wants your money… LOL.

What is more important? Money or Love?

My vote is on Love. Love can always be found. Money??? Not so

Today everything must have a warranty.

easy… and lives are wasted going down that street. Love you can take to the grave and beyond. It is always there if you aren't stupid.

Now you can get married and have a family and taste the richness of life's love… If you can keep it together. Every member of a family is looking for love. In good families that reassurance is always there. As is the Truth of life. For you must learn what Truth is. No truth and no power. No truth and no love.

There is a Love that is always there though we try to look the other way when it looks at us. Your most important function is to independently search out pain, hunger, injustice, and emptiness. Making you the bearer of hope when someone's pain is perceived and addressed with your loving assurance.

That is an act of love.

That is what everyone is called to do when they grow up.

Light the candles in the hearts of those lacking Love and the Truth.

A lot to think about.

Guaranteed.

Open Heart

They opened my heart and took a close look. It needed some love. I don't know if you consider a surgeon's scalpel a love object... LOL.

So in they went and left me with my lucky number. 321. 3 Stents, a double bypass, and a pacemaker. So my heart got another life and all is good 4 years later.

When they went in they couldn't see love.

How come the heart is where you feel love?

The surgeon can put it in his hands, and not feel the love that is really there... Big time love.

Breaks your heart when someone says they don't love you anymore. No surgeon's blade is inside, but it sure feels like surgery... When you don't feel love it is like they took your heart out. Your emotional and moral compass are missing. You are floundering in a sea of feelings. Needing a life (love) vest fast.

Where can you go to get love races through your mind. Stupid decisions lead one to dark places and addictions. Short remedies for the greater pain. Nowhere street.

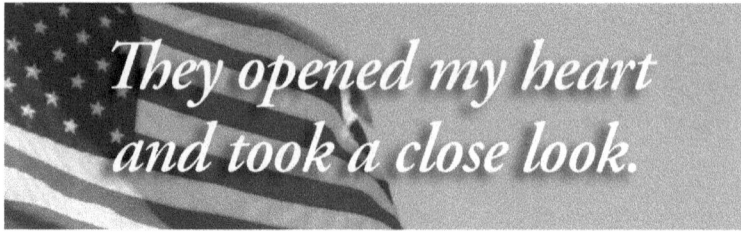
They opened my heart and took a close look.

But if you search for love in the right places and in the right people, you can find love again. The right church is a good place to start. A church can be anywhere. A person can be a church if you listen to their message of Hope, Truth, and Faith. There are so many people who devote themselves to the Truth found in their hearts. It is amazing how their hand can give you hope again. You have to have the courage to take it.

The "I'll pray for you." must be embraced and thought about.

Open your heart to alternatives.

An open heart is humble and hungry to help others.

Open your heart to this new calling. Let it fill with love... you'll feel the power.

If you have the courage.

Your choice.

Who said it was easy?

Sure beats dying with a closed heart...

The best surgeon's office I know says Jesus on the door.

Love That Dress

Instant smile for sure.

Just say "Love that dress!" and you get her attention.

Just find something to compliment and you become somebody.

"Love the way you think." is more intimate.

"Love the way you don't answer your phone." means your love wasn't true enough.

Maybe she didn't think you were sincere. Maybe she knew her dress wasn't that great. Nice try.

From hobbies to sports to travel to food…everyone has something they love. Passing time with them brings escape for the moment from work and responsibility. Look at the fortunes we spend on these favorite activities…

Sharing what you love about something is fun.

Sharing what you love about someone is a completely different ballgame. And every person has something to be loved for. Their looks, their courage, and their pain. Love changes the playing field always. Inject love and you find ways to surmount anything.

If you can create a smile, then you can create a cure.

We all have the ability to make a difference. All that one has to do is to be in a true loving state. It requires action. Turning concern into action. Turning compassion into action. Turning understanding into action. Just do it.

Be spontaneous when you see the pain of another. Get close and offer your hand and say you are really serious…that you really want to help… that you really are different than most people. A commitment to help brings a smile deep within in the both of you.

Caring companionship.

If you can create a smile, then you can create a cure.

Love conquers all.

"Love that new dress."

Reproductive Urge

Now this is a really tricky title.

The history of man is rife with the impacts of reproductive urges.

You know, that feeling that wells up in your heart and blinds you to sanity.

Sometimes it is called love.

Otherwise it is the old reproductive urge like a Joker in our own personal Batman movie. Wars were fought by Kings wanting Queens.

How did the world get so many people? One hell of an urge??? We all know about the physical side of the urge…each one of us being a consequence of an urge that was good or that was bad. Depends on the actual spirit of the moment. Taking??? Or Giving???

But there is more to the urge, for it provides existence. It is the glue of creation.

All the good that man does comes from how he respects this

Now this is a really tricky title.

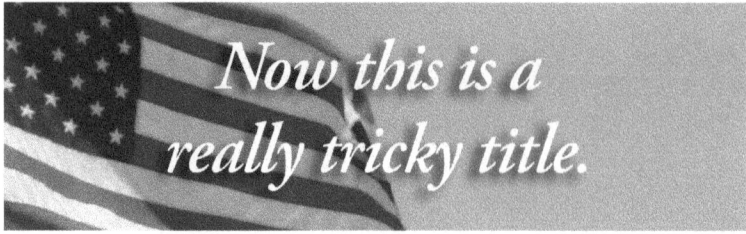

amazing gift. "With this ring I thee wed". We all clap, and cry, and hope for the best...

There are countries where love is a travesty. Where rape is love. Where reproduction puts an unbearable burden on a child and deep degradation to the mother. How can she be asked to ever find love?

We now must look at the central issue of our times. And that is the degradation of values. Is there anything we value? Innocence is being stolen by the cell phone. The word "No" is contested... especially when "feelings" come first. A father used to be the "No" man. But more and more fathers are not around, abrogating authority to the abandoned mother. "No", this is not right.

Who can teach "values" when schools can't use the word? When the word "good" is not allowed as it has morality underpinnings. To define good one must define evil. Our schools are not up to it. Churches are mocked as citadels of right wing extremism. Universities neuter Christianity with comparative religion history courses. God no longer exists other than as a curious distraction in histories.

The Middle East will bring us down. We have lost our resolve and we ignore the importance of concrete values. Lawyers and bureaucracies deflect and delay any solution.

The reproductive urge now has many laws to protect it.

As long as it feels good.

Chase it while you can.

Reproduce and don't look back. LOL.

Darkroom

In the old days cameras had real film in them.

The photo negatives were taken into a darkroom to be developed.

The photo paper was suspended in a special liquid until the exposure brightened into a picture, then brought out and hung until dry.

Then this memory was framed under glass so all could see forever.

Some frames were real expensive depending how much the picture was loved. All this beauty saved by the darkroom. Some pictures are so uniquely beautiful that you cannot take your eyes off them. You love them. Pictures don't have to be of pretty things. Sometimes the ugly needs to be seen so Truth is not ignored.

Say "darkroom" 20 times holding your lower lip.

Hmmm... sounds like darkwomb...

Two people lost in love create a new picture that gets developed in the dark womb of the mother. It is an astounding event in its sensuality. But more so in the creation of life. A miracle that will never be understood except in a biological sense. A child will

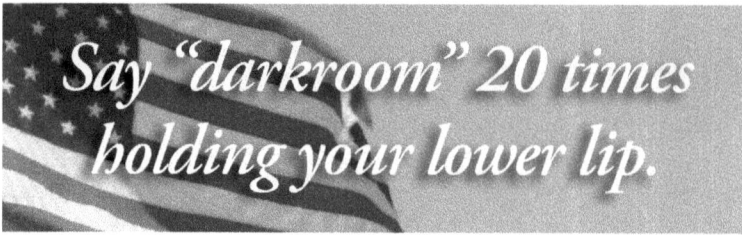

emerge from this dark space and one day become a lover. You see, love creates love. Astounding.

Love is meant to be unequivocally pure. Only Truth can give love value. Sin tries to destroy love. Vanity and insecurity try to destroy love. We are our own Supreme Court which decides the choice we make. Respecting love or disrespecting love. Pretending otherwise makes us a fool.

The best possible feeling one can find in life is loving someone. But to love someone else, one must put them above yourself. To love means to serve. To love means to help someone. Opening one's eyes to the pain and suffering all around that is hidden to most. Compassion, encouragement, and holding is the mandate of love. Otherwise you will never know real love.

It is kind of like giving your life up for someone. Like throwing yourself on a grenade to protect your buddy. Pure love.

As we develop our understanding of love our life can evolve into something more unique and special than we ever thought. By helping as many we can, however small the gesture, we get to know love.

Our nation was founded on certain love principles.

Created by a man who threw himself on a wooden grenade to save us.

Thank God that picture was developed.

Wright Angle

A shipwright builds ships.

A playwright writes plays.

A sky writer leaves messages in the skies.

The Wright Brothers had to come first.

Wonder what a lovewright does?

We all want to be a wrighter and create something meaningful.

I like to write to flesh out what has meaning.

I like to write about things that are right. Because if you are right you cannot be wrong.

There is so much in the world, in our nation, and in our families that is not right. I think we need a lovewrighter to get our attention.

To write about Love.

To write about Truth.

We need to know the Gospel truth to upright our lives. And we

Wonder what a lovewright does?

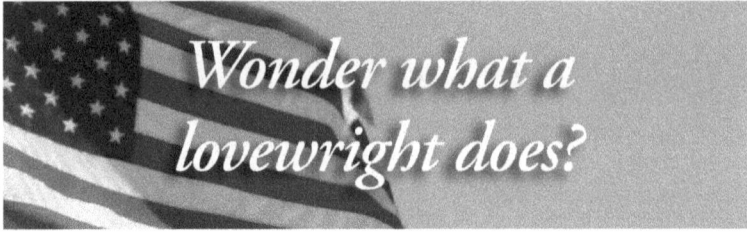

all know that is the truth…except we keep it quiet. We want to avoid attention. We are abdicating our reason for being. We are each called to bring Love where it is needed. That means getting off our intellectual fannies and doing something that matters. And it only matters if you are doing it for someone else.

To be a lovewright we have to find the right perspective to view things. We need to go to the right and to our core historical values and stand for them out loud. Call me a right wing extremist if you want, but I have had a blessed life and it is time to give back. But with active love, not checks. Claim your lovewright. Just do it.

The right angle is bringing others to the right. They will love you. Rightly so.

The rightest angle is over your wright shoulder and up.

Funny, a Cross is made up of right angles…..

WWIII

WWI was really bad if you were on the ground.

WWII ended with the atomic bomb.

WWIII might end with an EMP bomb. Electro Magnetic Pulse.

It fries electrical grid works.... So no lights, no refrigerators, no nothing electric.

No cell phone systems. All gone.

It is being debated.

Our founding fathers devised a Constitution that was based on unanimous bedrock values.

WWIII has already begun and we started it... We let it happen while media pundits over-analyzed everything while ignoring evil. Evil can't really exist say the professors.

Does good exist? What is good? And what is evil? It cannot be discussed as it is what right wing extremists talk about. So what is good and what is evil is no longer taught in schools.

Values. What are they? Are they important? Who defines them? For starters most original government buildings have Christian

WWIII has already begun and we started it...

quotes on them. "We as a nation must not forget that God is the author of our liberty, for if we do we shall lose it."

What our schools are doing is neutering Christianity. Political correctness, our chosen cancer, is destroying our ability to make decisions.

The American Flag is being debated as it suggests freedom and right wing ideology. Patriotism is frowned on when it may not be Politically Correct.

A school I went to sent out their PC Christmas greeting prefaced with "Holiday Wishes" ...??? Huuuhhh? Am I missing something?

There are no Values courses in schools or universities. The strength of our nation came from its cornerstone Christian values. Great moral fiber. Oops, "moral" suggests morality... another taboo subject.

If we love our family, if we love our country, if we love our freedom, we had better change our ways soon.

Where we came from was a special love. A love of Christianity and her "love one another" ethos was the engine of our success. We have helped more people than any other nation. We were able to do it because we were love-centric. Injustice was attacked. Now it is just a news item.

The war has started and we can't see it.

We had better figure out what we love fast.

Before it is too late.

Godspeed America.

Peace On Earth

WWIII is inevitable.

Look at the 1,000's of years of conflicts where leaders tried to negotiate.

It got them nowhere.

Treaties signed and broken.

Deceit in infinite assurances.

Temporary peace only came through strength and action that wasn't hesitant.

What is the expression?? "He who hesitates is lost."

When you don't know what to do you hesitate, ponder, debate. And pass a law. LOL.

Yet, this is more about us and our decision making machine.

A person of conviction is formed through strong moral values and hard work.

The sad news is that we no longer expose our kids to hard work. You can dismiss it all you want... but through hard work one

WWIII is inevitable.

learns and earns pride, dignity, and knowledge. Don't spare the rod… life doesn't.

A father has to be in the equation. If not, love never was. Love is unselfish. Kids need to learn to be unselfish. They need to exercise more muscles than their keyboard fingertips.

We need our youth to be strong so they CAN defend us.

We need youth to experience the military. It should be mandatory. Pride can be found there… Not on self-congratulatory social networking.

We need leadership.

We need the leadership from those formed in love not in indulgement.

Love is at the center of all solutions.

Love requires living in Truth.

How many of us can say that we do?

You want peace on earth?

Then get honest and begin to put Love in every moment.

When it comes from your heart don't be hesitant.

If you don't get it… keep trying

Don't quit on love.

Global Raping

Scientists have refused to address global raping as a possible source of global warming (GW). If we disrespect life and women it is easier to disrespect the earth.

Global Raping (GR) does more harm than we think.

We like everything tidy and non-confrontational.

When the Oscar is given and the speech is about the danger from global warming I want to choke.

There are so many nightmare conditions and causes to be addressed and GW is just not the worst. It just falls into a sub-category of GR.

Women and children continue to be abused in horrific numbers. The male of the Middle East shamefully embraces women's abuse by hiding it behind black robes and closed doors. Where in the world did their distorted intellects make it so black is white... and rape a solution?

Here in the USA there are penalties for abuse and rape. Though our lawyers do their best to exonerate the guilty... Shamefully...

Global Raping (GR) does more harm than we think.

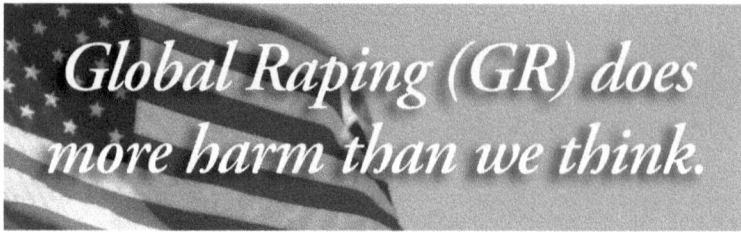

Something has gone wrong with us. We don't like uncomfortable feelings so we send a Letter to the Editor who prints and quasi-absolves us by just printing it. Values are obstacles to feelings... Get the drift?

Our pundits analyze us to sleep with intricate spins on the surface facts. But beneath it all is our self-serving ignoring of the primary role of love. Making babies is an exalting experience. The sensation and intimacy is meant to glorify love. The intense intimacy is the motor of desire. But... this feel-good pursuit abdicates Truth and commitment. Making love is a contract to Truth and a future and a family that should be holy ground. But it is just laughed at.

The sublime form of rape is the deceit of the moment. Where love is not Truth.

It is politically incorrect to talk about cultural rape.... because... just because... we may be equally guilty.

What is wrong with the old rules of holding the door open for a woman? The notion that the man protects the woman... and the child?

Why can't we fight this war and take this disrespect head-on?

Because a nation supplies us with oil, we turn our heads from its abuse and rape.

The podium of the Oscars is a place for actors to show us humility and leadership.

And because they glorify the beauty of women, and make fortunes off their beauty… should they not lead the charge?

How about a concert against "Global Raping"

We are subtly raping ourselves if we don't.

Me Universe

A teenager named Ricky and his brother Scotty were in my office.

Great laughter.

Home schooled.

Wow!... Were they amazing!

Their mom had to really love them to put all that successful effort into it. They got an old fashioned education and were knowledgeable and bright...history, English, languages... scary... and mannered and respectful and fun. Go figure?? Ran circles around the public school system.

We talked about helping others. They get it.

And how the universe of so many kids is their feelings and what makes them feel good. Only that. Love of nothing else but self. And with the infinite support of social networks and cell phones they feel infallible. Ricky said, "Their world and thinking is so small. They know love of things... but they've lost track of family love."

Kids have created their own love walls to keep out any unwanted intrusions. Values and things like patriotism are easily dismissed

Thanks Ricky and Scotty.

as irrelevant. The Pledge of Allegiance is long gone. Headphones are as indispensable as underwear. Cell phone screens feed biases and irrelevant banter into brains.

A new spelling?? "Celf Love"... love it?? "Celf Love"... LOL.

The "Universe of Me" has always been there, but in the new era of technology more control over more things is more automated, more depersonalized, and more seductive. Youth is being raped by technology. It feels so good. Keyboards are the slot machines of the now. Sugar for the brain.

As we meandered through our discussion, we kept coming back to love. It had to be more than self-destructive.

They knew that helping others, that serving others was the best high. Getting love away from self actually created new unimagined freedoms. Pride that defined manhood with quiet confidence. Helping the poor. Helping anyone in need.

Ricky and Scotty emoted dignity behind all the laughter.

One says "How low can you go?" Keep loving self and you will find out. "How high can you go?" The sky is the limit if love is given. Every small unselfish act can be really important to someone. It feels really good... makes you smile inside.

You see, these kids know. They already have a PHD in Values.

They have grown up around lost alcoholics and drug abusers. They have seen the destruction self-love can lead to. The terrible waste of souls lost... without love.

You see their dad runs a homeless shelter.

Don't you love it?

Love University.

Thanks Ricky and Scotty.

Love Bust

"Hey you... pull over.

Get out of the car.

Hands on the roof.

What's in that bag in your pocket??

Hands behind you."

Handcuffed.

"White powder. Sure isn't baby powder?? Eh??"

We wonder how and why so many succumb to drugs and alcohol. It has to be with aloneness. With not feeling loved. Get high and you can love yourself.

The quickest road to tragedy and self-worth destruction. There is no answer with the next high. Doom. Dirty clothes. Nights somewhere but nowhere.

You could call it a Love Bust, except there is no love.

A different kind of Love Bust happens when love is given to those in need of love. Kindness, politeness, truthfulness are all gifts

Hey you... pull over.

of respect to someone else. We can feel the true high in serving others. When you get that mindset you find a new freedom and an infinite amount of small opportunities to make a difference. Just a "You look nice." Or a "How about letting me help you?"... and, of course, not taking no for an answer. Carrying out the garbage... or better yet, the neighbor's garbage. Eyes always alert for opportunities to help in some small way.

We can break the cycles of hurt and take them to the Love Dump. That is the dump where you take the pain and discomfort of others... It makes the Love Dump a big mountain. Love does so much good. It is a testament of what man is capable of... if he is willing to pray and stay where he is needed.

So next time you are out, bust up someone else's despair with compassion.

Be a Love Detective and make the best kind of busts.

Love Busts Rock.

Love Or Consequences

Truth or Consequences, New Mexico.

Talk about being nowhere… Go Google it.

It was named after a famous TV show in the 1950's.

30 Miles east is a spaceport.

The show was about answering questions with the truth and the correct answer to get the prize.

Bet you don't know where I am going…

Supposed we changed one word in the name??? Truth to Love.

Sounds like if you don't know real love you can't tell the truth…? You just aren't there yet.

There are consequences to Love. It is our choice how to treat it.

Our first feelings as a kid are not fully formed… but we do innately love our mom, our dad, our sister, our brother… In later years we really love them. Love as a part of our life is formed.

Attraction, passion, and intimate friendship enters our lives in our teens and drives so much of our private energies and distraction.

Truth or Consequences, New Mexico.

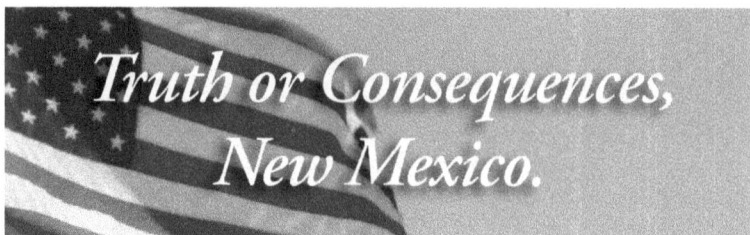

Love is beautiful as it makes one feel unselfish. You just want to care for the other person. As the mother at birth. After the joyous pain.

The greed of sex can often replace the innocence and power of love. Self-gratification kills growth. One is blinded by the amazing sensations of the bodies. There are major consequences now. People can get really hurt in the cultures of gratification. Memories of hurt that never are forgotten.

Love or consequences? Love is the path to Truth. Truth can only be found with humility and compassion. If you are lucky you will find that helping others yields a pureness of satisfaction. It is no longer self-centric. You become who you were meant to be. You can't if you are lost in self and things.

Life is not about a golden retriever kind of love... yet ... maybe... you can learn that their trusting love is what you are searching for in another. That trust that allows you to be really free to help any person in need that crosses your path. Not with money but by giving respect. None of us are any better than the other save for circumstances, pain, and loveless journeys.

We know there are consequences.

The worst are from its abuse.

The most wonderful are from its innocence.

Found only in Truth.

Love or consequences...?

Godspeed.

Ricky

From the deepest recesses of my soul, tears rise as my cheek presses next to Ricky's.

Kiss…… tears private… life's breath ceases.

You could say it is only a dog.

But it is more than that.

It is love.

Love we all feel when anyone dies.

He was a perfect golden retriever, though red. I found him from a breeder way back in the woods years ago. Took him and his sister. I had found Lucy there a year prior.

God, it hurts. Love is so pure. How often we disrespect it. How in the world does a mother ever accept a loss? How does a child feel when a parent passes?

Is not LOVE the greatest TRUTH!!

Every life slain by evil and selfishness ends up in tears. Don't tell me that tears are not the most honest of bodily reactions. Sometimes they don't stop. When your gut meets your heart.

Ricky loved to swim.

Today reminds me how angry I am about the abuse of love, of women, of children. Honesty and humility and strength and identity are the byproducts of love. So whenever these are abused the pain will be great and often unseen or admitted. Conceit festers as one tries to protect self-image. Selfishness takes over. Silent tears abound unknown to the person.

Life is all about finding Truth. Truth can only be found in true love... which is the unselfish serving of others.

Why are dogs so damned special?? Is it because they can just love without condition unlike us? Mistreat them and you lose. And that means you don't know diddly about life, love, or truth.

Abuse love and you lose.

I did once... and hurt many.

Forgiveness is not easy for anyone.

But forgiveness also comes from above.

Where Love was born.

Ricky loved to swim.

So did I.

Evil

To many of us evil is evil.

Yet to many, evil is just a subset of explanations and rationalization. It cannot exist. Crime might, but criminals are the new victims and the real victims are forgotten.

It is not politically correct to use the word "evil". It is moralizing and forces one to define what is "good". You can't speak of being moral as it borders on preaching, which is taboo today. You can't tell someone else what to do...???

There are no Values courses in schools or universities. A teacher cannot teach or mention values, good or bad. Families are dysfunctional as is our educational system.

Social networks have no bounds. What is moral is attacked by tweets.

We are weak and don't see it. Our children are being raised on meaningless vague conditions. Lawyers are having a field day protecting the inane.

To many of us evil is evil.

We are weak in our core. The Middle East sees us as broken and evil. They have so much video to support the dark side of capitalism. Beheading Christians is an act of war not a news blog. Our leaders talk and talk and talk. Don't they see that something horrific is taking shape that is larger than our capacity to control?

If we love our family, if we love our country, if we love our freedom.... we had better change our ways soon.

Or evil will win.

Ear Love

Our ears are always alert to our name being said by another person.

Ears physically don't stand up or move like a dog's. A dog survives by being alert to everything around him. They even warn us. Woof!

We, like them, try to listen to everything being said.

We have to know if someone likes us or is criticizing us.

That is the amazing appeal of texting and social networks.

We want so badly to be liked and do our best not to show it!!

And we love our ears when the news is good.

"Did she really say that??" is our radar going active as we track down the truth. Going to friends for more detail. Ear driven self-preservation even goes before global warming on the priority list.

Then there is music. A feast for the ears and the within. Love songs. Country ballads. Piano. Italian tenors. Classical. Jazz. Top 40. Every generation has its special music to bring one back.

We love our ears when the news is good.

There are high-end expensive speakers and amplifiers that cost in the 10's of thousands of dollars in the pursuit of hearing the exact beauty of music. Boy... do we love to listen. Anytime, anywhere. Bluetooth unleashed. Sirius attached. Ear buds deployed. We listen.

But there is another side to listening. While not talking.

It is listening to the other person. Not interrupting. Respecting them with your attention and silence.

We want to be heard when we have something to say. Without listening to another they won't listen to us. Listening is a form of serving someone else. We make the other person feel good when we listen. When they are finished and we have absorbed their need we offer heartfelt comment. A bond is formed in being honest and respectful. A trust that can be built on. This is the gift and power of listening.

Pain needs to be shared.

Hands need to be held in the search for relief and truth.

Maybe we can change holding hands to "holding ears"?

Nations should listen to their poor.

Many don't bother.

Evil flourishes, not love.

Now that is an earful.

Freedom

Let Freedom Ring.

LFR is not a matter to LOL about.

Let Flags Rise? LFR?

Let's not forget where we came from and who we were meant to be.

The love of freedom lies silently in every heart, regardless of religion or wealth.

The poor know chains. They know want. They know they have no freedom.

When will women be freed from the oppression of male bigotry and selfishness?

The Middle East denigrates woman. Servitude and constant private fear of the next moment. Freedom facaded. Slavery in a veil.

We in America are free to protest, free to love anything in most any way. One could say we are testing the limits of freedom. The internet has allowed freedom of access to all that is good and all

Dark clouds are ahead as black flags wave.

that is bad. There is no DIA (Department of Internet Access). Underage children are travelling the internet. Adults are salting their time with pander.

Freedom to the world is the American Flag. Our history of freeing the oppressed. World wars endured to protect freedom. The stones of Arlington National Cemetery attest.

We love freedom. We love McDonald's. Choice is so abundant here. Freedom to go anywhere anytime. Amazing. So beautiful. Races and cultures complementing one another in our Democracy.

Love, Love, Love Freedom. The smallest of minorities are free to make big noise for their concerns and wishes. Amazing. Freedom.

Yet, it is slipping from our hands like sand in our palms. We are losing the values we shed so much blood for. Political correctness is neutering our freedom to mature. Our freedom is becoming narrowed as we legislate the fine print of behavior.

It is as if we no longer love freedom enough to fight for it. We want it without blood. Does this not tell us something about a lack of commitment?

Dark clouds are ahead as black flags wave.

Funny, black is colorless.

It represents no freedom.

No red, no white, no blue.

Just beheadings.

Let Freedom Ring?

Single Mom

Was a mom meant to be a dad?

The number of single moms in the USA exceeds 10,000,000. Maybe 15 million.

40% of all children born are born to unwed mothers. The racial comparisons are devastating. Education has not worked in the schools or homes.

What the "hope for lasting love" promised has been dashed by the rush to sensual fulfillment. This is expensive and costing the nation too much in dollars and time… lifetimes.

Love is the most powerful allure.

The perversion of love and its ridicule in media is profound. Making light of the serious has crippled futures. Children raised by damaged role models…with part time fathers or mothers…

Love has been neutered by self-centeredness.

Love has become play. In the sandbox of the senses. Childlike we avoid responsibility.

Was a mom meant to be a dad?

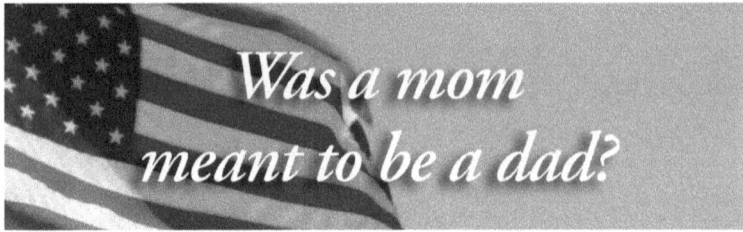

We pay women less. Cultures cloak women in black and fear. Abuse of all kinds is sadly ignored by media and politicians, our so-called leaders.

In a way, most single moms are the heroes as their love for their child has them working long hours in order to provide. Alone with their private thoughts of self-doubt and unseen tears. And pillows clutched tightly.

The sexual revolution started in the 1960's and created a 10 fold increase in single motherhood.

So it was a failure.

It was naïve and stupid.

Religion was not wrong. Nobody listens.

Media fed the beast and abandoned value driven programming. Media stood for nothing but profits... at any cost.

How do single moms teach love when they are not home or there to pick up the kids?

What do we stand for anymore??

How do we teach love that endures all of life's challenges and diversions?

It's there in some pews and in the hearts of the inspired.

When you say "love you" start meaning it.

He did.

Conception

Who conceived conception?

When was the beginning?

Doesn't love have something to do with it???

Could it be in the mutual twinkling of eyes for the first time?

The first moment of attraction?

The promise of a dreamed love that was worth giving your life to?

The strong desire to take care of someone?

Overpowering feelings. Senses heightened. A taste of truth in the promise of true love.

What happens next can destroy the life of both if the fulfillment of the passion is taken lightly. Where lies may enter.

Fertilization moments shared. Genuine smiles.

The next days and months hold signals of commitment or not.

The stomach still grows regardless. A human child is forming. From inception?

Who conceived conception?

That is your private perspective but a very, very important one.

The mother is the awesome server of this new life. She gets to know the pain of birth. And what mothers have borne for thousands and thousands of years. The private beauty and awe of a life is hers.

Conception sort of applies to all that we do. If we truly love something we will give our all to it. Be it a sport or be it helping others. Or the design of something. Or the brush of the artist. The first moment of the formation of an idea is special and can propel one to greatness if protected.

Values were created to make life orderly and fair and good. What has value is taught by our every act. We are observed all the time. People form their values by observing what is important to others.

Goodness is the soil of conception.

Self cannot be the fertilizer.

Nothing grows from self-centeredness.

Who are the people we truly admire? Not the celebrities. It is the people who give their lives to helping others, to being fair, to standing up for good… to feeling the silent cries of the poor.

Conception is a miracle and the greatest of all gifts.

Birth is our diamond.

To Whom do you want to give it to be cut??

Tough Love

Love is so easy to find.

It's not that tough.

Real love… pure love, not selfish love.

Love feels so good.

It is at its best when it's honest.

Look at all we do for our kids because we love them… Our love is teaching them what we think of love. What we think about honesty, what we think about good.

Good love makes for good families.

Except that we have forgotten how love is supposed to work.

No one follows any rules anymore. Only the rules of self. The rules of "I want this".

Who is there to say "no"? The police?? Is that not too late??

Love is not tough. But toughness has to be brought back when love is abused. Manners and respect are good products of good love. If a kid or person is disrespectful then all we have left is tough love.

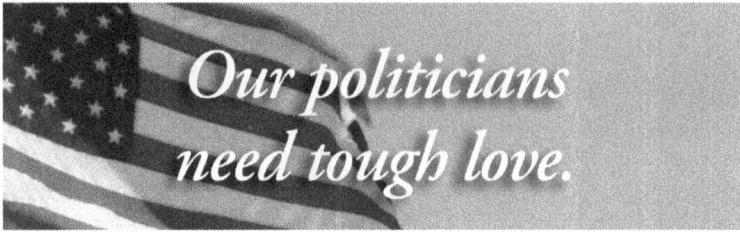
Our politicians need tough love.

We must correct behavior by putting a price on misbehavior. Not jail, but more serious impositions by parent and teacher. Cell phones taken away for a week… that is a real contemporary spanking!

Screams and yells for naught. Too bad. Tough love is love. Tough love keeps even worse from happening. Clear messages must be sent about right and wrong. Values must be valuable again. They must be taught in the homes and schools again. Our future and our survival depends on tough love.

There are cultures out there where a hand is cut off because you do not follow the rules. Where women and girls are slaves to false truths and horror.

We must strengthen our young with the repercussion of tough love before it is too late.

Our military is where tough love has been perfected in the loud yells of the drill instructor. Where wandering minds are given order and purpose. Where pride in following the rules is alive again.

It is tough to learn love the right way. To be an example of the right way. To be respected for being a protector of what this nation stands for. What an honor!

Tough love makes our Flag have meaning.

Stop quitting and start loving the right stuff.

Our politicians need tough love.

Who is going to give it to them?

Biscuits & Gravy

Is there anything worse than this?

White flour, white sausage gravy…both thick and mushy.

Begging for more salt and the fork.

It stares up at you from the plate.

Trying to be sensual.

Your choice. Almost like… choosing life or death?

Why do seemingly insignificant choices have the potential to do great harm? Our day is full of choices that can have an impact on ourselves and others.

The menu is colorful and beautifully printed. Like makeup on a model.

Do we always think before we lift a fork… or does the appeal of this entrée overwhelm judgement? LOL.

Cuban sandwiches or drive thru everything makes it all so easy. Hey… we drive thru life and make quick choices which take their toll over time.

Is there anything worse than this?

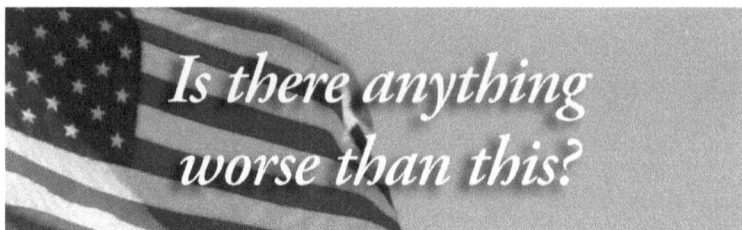

Our world and our families are facing tough choices.

Will we be lean and ready?

What does it take to take on the evil that is headed our way?

As a nation are we getting too fat in body and spirit? Are values and time-proven rules being ignored? Is the Constitution being pushed aside?

Is the love of freedom in jeopardy?

Dads have left their families. Politicians have left to be swallowed by bureaucracy and special interests. Our leadership is protected by infinite fine print and call forwarding robots. No wonder we turn to biscuits and gravy when all is beginning to taste so bad.

How do you teach a child not to do things that you know are wrong? Do we find an excuse? Do we pass the buck to the internet? Can Google solve our woes?

Hello? There is really nothing wrong with spanking. Tough love for sure. But it certainly is a lesser punishment than taking away the cell phone!!!

Biscuits & Gravy are waiting for you.

Bet the devil created it.

Which we will deny.

Who else do we deny?

Our Father who art...

Mother's Day

Today is Mother's Day.

Mom has been gone for close to 20 years.

As each year passes I remember more and more about how she molded me.

We all are gardens that moms planted their seeds in.

Encouraging us to be beautiful, to find things she wanted us to.

When our heads first emerged from her body in her scream of pain and excruciating joy... the journey began.

Hopefully a dad was there to hold your hand and hers.

A mother teaches one about love the way she wants it to be.

Unconditionally offered. As she serves us into our first light.

Embedded in love is the birth of Truth. She wants us each to be good and to champion Truth. Moms want our lives to be better, as we are guided towards marriage and making her grandchildren have it even better.

That would make our mom proud...

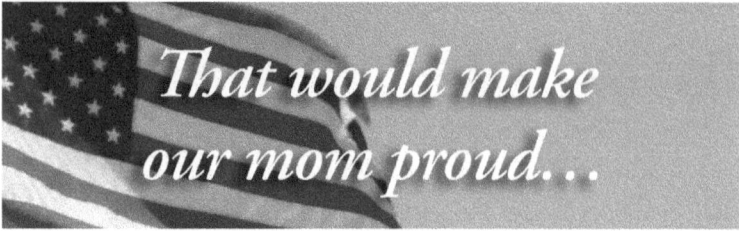

Truth and values become attacked as soon as the mother loses control. The corridors of high schools and the halls of the internet intertwine in cell phone frenzy as mothers' tears form.

When we mature we begin to see how hard mom tried in spite of all the forces against her. She offered so much advice that was true and unheard by our ear bud blocked ears... listening only to music of our immediate fancy.

Hey, I have a new prayer.... "Our mother who art in heaven..."

Some mothers are dealt difficult hands when dad has left. When there is no money. Or when she wants to run away and does.

We feel everything that our mother feels in some sublime way. Often not knowing that we do. Silent seeds of doubt and insecurity making our deeply private existence even more complex.

You see, deep down beneath it all, we really care about mom. She tried to pass on the Truth that love is only about serving someone else. That love cannot co-exist with selfishness. There are always people during every day that we can help...be it with a compassionate word or a small helpful act. That would make our mom proud...

So on this day every year let your mom know you love her.

Wherever she is.

For she was our first love.

Unconditional

Is anything unconditional anymore??

Different interpretations are so numerous you don't know which one will go to court.

When we fall in love one gets the feeling of the power of "unconditional". But then there is the "PRENUP"… LOL.

Today fine print is absolving everyone from responsibility. Everything has become conditional.

Yet somewhere deep in the womb…unconditional love exists. At creation. As seeds are fertilized. There is something special going on that we must respect.

Creation is special. Think about it. When the artist sees a vision and his brush makes something unique. Rembrandt? Van Gogh? Monet? And on into today.

The Internet was created by man. The camera. The automobile. French bread.

Love was poured into the best creations, unconditionally.

Conditions create abortions.

Is anything unconditional anymore??

Conditions create failure.

Conditions create mediocrity.

Who created water? OK... we kinda have explanations for the moon and the planets...kinda...And then there are the galaxies seen and the yet to be seen. One's imagination comes to a brick wall. How can all this be? Let's drop our egos and opinions for a moment. How did all this stuff come into balance? The beauty of science only gets us so far. The brick wall is Faith.

We get lost in our earthly satisfactions and in the wars of ideology and terror.

But when one looks up it gets confusing. How can earth be so small compared to the universe? Our mind ponders it only momentarily as one anticipates dinner.... LOL.

If I were a surgeon deep in heart surgery....Is not the complexity of the human body as mind-boggling as the universe? Because we cannot understand it all we don't bother. As we have other more satisfying distractions.

Yet, something unconditional is at the root of it all. Beyond science there is Faith. Everything becomes clear and more beautiful with God. So much coherent good is done in His name.

His love is unconditional. We don't get it. But if we don't try we will never be who we could have become.

Each of us a star in the farthest galaxy.

Bringing light to a person in need, be it a friend or stranger....

Imagine a day in which all that you do is unconditional.

As long as it is good.

Be a star.

Godspeed.

Never Enough

Why is it that when you find something you like you can never get enough of it?

Different interpretations are so numerous: Pasta, wine, golf, scuba, travel, shopping… and on and on. For every one of us there is at least one thing you love and can't get enough. Family dinners if you can get the family together and if there is a cell phone basket… LOL.

Today, all can't get enough of texting. Enough of the good or the bad on the internet. You can never get enough of what you love even if you are an Olympic gold medal winner.

Love this, love that. Some form of love is at the center. Seems like you just can't avoid loving something. Every human on this planet past and present respects and/or needs love.

If you don't love yourself you will abuse it. Drugs, alcohol all prove how much you want love but can't get it. Love is at the center of our existence from first breath to last.

The ultimate feelings from love come from serving and caring for

Today we can't get enough of texting.

others… more than self. When you fall in love and get married the power of love makes perfection seem possible.

Helping the poor, the less fortunate in any small way on any day will give you that quiet feeling inside your private self of having done good… of having loved.

Do I want to say an orgasm of unselfishness?

"Love makes the world go 'round." Get it?

Evil is always fighting love. Sadistic abuse and denigration and terror are prevalent today. Some say we look the other way.

If we love truth and can't get enough of it then we have the tool to win. Love trumps reason and evil. There is a war ahead. We have to want Truth and never get enough of it.

Love what you can do.

Love who you can be.

Die to self.

And bow to Thee.

Apology

Who in the world wants to apologize?

It is like admitting defeat.

Remember back when your mom or dad said "Now Christopher I want you to apologize to the baby sitter for making a mess."

Huuhh?? I was trying to help her clean up.

"Christopher?!!"

"Ok, but I had to finish the TV show. Sorry…"

If you love your mom you will fess up. What is it about love that forces out the truth?

Our moms loved us so much from day one that we had to be honest with her. "If you love me just tell me the truth." "Fair enough?"

Sometimes when we are older we just wait for time to pass so it is forgotten. At work or at home we don't want to admit we might be wrong. Apologizing is asking someone for forgiveness. Pride takes a little hit.

Who in the world wants to apologize?

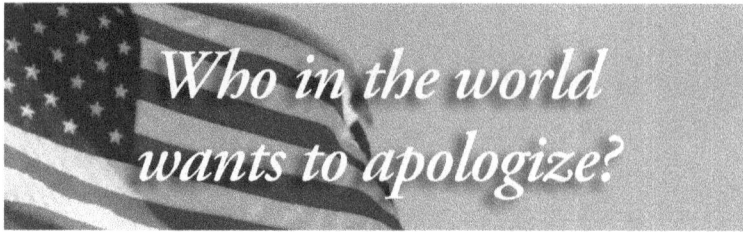

Sometimes we are not wrong, but have to apologize anyway for the better good. That is always a private "forever" decision. But when you forgive someone you know you are making their world better….and yours.

Loving truth is the path to protecting love. This is a heavy statement. Think about it. Loving truth is the path to protecting love.

Apologies take private courage. Only you will know. These are the front lines of the battle for truth.

Forgiveness is such a fantastic reward.

We can't stay in love with someone if we don't live in truth with them.

Apologies are the glue of truth.

Only one person never had to apologize.

Bar Maid

Barmaids flourished in old England and raised the standard pint to the customer. I like to call that "raising the standards"... Like, drink your beer and everyone feels better.

And nothing like having a barmaid hand it to you. Kinda classy.

Assaults on and the diminishment of standards are bringing our country and our world into a confused state of direction. By catering to every opinion we are catering to none. We are lowering all kinds of standards so as not to make it difficult anymore. Therein lies the peril. The Middle East certainly sees it...

To digress, why are SEALs and Special Operations Forces so good? Why are we counting on them so much these days? Because to be one you have to pass the highest of standards. Really tough and painful. Frightening to most. This excellence comes from punishing endurance standards on land and in sea. Young men giving it their all. They get to know pride from achievement. From rising to higher standards. Where quitting is not an option.

Don't we need to raise the bar in our families and in our businesses? Ethics and integrity must be part of all endeavor. To

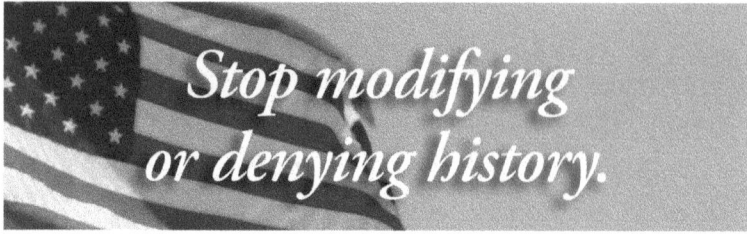

do this, values must be redefined that acknowledge our traditions. There is nothing wrong with traditional definitions of good and evil. Enough with the sensitivity trainings that makes one afraid to say anything…

"Good" must be taught in schools and in living rooms. Church teachings are an asset, not an illusion. Finding the right church is part of raising your moral bar. Parents must get tough. Teachers must get tough. Politically correct school boards need to lead, not follow the PC bigotry. There should be a Values 101 course in every grade and college. The sensitivities of the few must not trump the needs of the majority.

The legal profession has been writing too much fine print to protect their insurance portfolios. Why can't they show more moral leadership? Frivolous suits have to be denied. They are clogging up the legal system. Raise the bar on the bar. Yes the state bar exams have to be about fairness to Truth and what is best, not most profitable.

Politicians have lowered their bar so much that it is not worth discussing.

We need barmaids of Truth. Let them help us pray in school again.

Let the flag be saluted.

Let our Constitution be taught unabridged.

Stop modifying or denying history.

There is nothing wrong with God but us.

We have made too many gods… Like the Romans 1,000's of years ago.

I'm going out for a pint.

See ya at the bar.

Don't ya love it?

Being Used

If you care about finding real love, then you are vulnerable to love that is not real.

The initial glance hints of the impossible.

A whisper inside the heart sends a pulse through the body.

Hope and dreams collide…

Love is in the air????

Any small additional signal makes one stumble forward… closer.

If it is not genuine then you become prey.

You pray not to be prey.

The power of love is glorified everywhere. All media shows physical perfections. Abundant happiness tied to marketing ploys. We are being circled by the vultures of disingenuous images of love. We spend countless years of time absorbing media created love. We are being used.

We must challenge every assertion of love to test its lasting strength and purity. Isn't that what we are after anyway??

Being used is an awful feeling.

Misrepresenting love is the greatest of all unseen crimes. We are all vulnerable to love. It is so precious. It is so easily abused.

False assertions of love to satisfy the moment are egregious. When discovered, the heart ache is deadly. Shattering someone's life and innocence. It is selfish and criminal.

Being used is an awful feeling.

How can you trust again?

Where do you go for relief?... Family?

Where you go is where you still have trust.

Maybe on your knees?

Heart Valve

A friend lost his daughter to complications from heart valve surgery.

Your heart goes to your gut and the painful private journey begins.

The love of a father knows no solace.

The mind blanks in agony.

I had heart surgery, double by-pass, stents, and pacemaker. Has added a few years to this old man. Life is precious. I gotta write for my daughters.

As blood flows through the miracle of life, our heart, do we fully appreciate the complexity and love that created it?

Are there valves to love? What happens when we cannot love anymore? Is that not death? It certainly becomes the playground of evil.

When we can love freely... Not by loving things, money, possessions, or lust... We find that our life has meaning. That we are truly alive. Ever felt this?? Complete freedom because you love.

Love means helping others, not the mirror.

Some will die.

It is the greatest gift of life. It starts with parents. And is even better if the parent can teach one about all the wonderful kinds of love. Even a puppy can teach you. You will not let anything harm it.

The valves of love can shrink when abused. When you lie about love. What happens?? You slowly die to substance abuse, alcohol, lying, and self-gratification. Go to homeless shelters and rehabs or jails to see what a broken love valve can do.

For them it will take major surgery. Some won't survive it. Some will die.

You had better have the best heart surgeon.

You had better have the best love surgeon.

I think He wears white.

And operates unseen.

To those on their knees.

Swimsuit Issue

How many guys can't wait for it to come out in the Spring?

They love looking at it. Politically correct for the most part. Not like the other magazines they may love looking at. LOL. They have no issue with that. Many deplore out loud, but in private??... They have no issue. Oops... except the one they are reading.

For many, especially women, they have an "issue" with this issue.

It seems that "issues" are getting prime coverage in our media these days.

Differing opinions become "issues".

What is it about the word "issue" that has become so important??

We can no longer say something is wrong, just plain wrong.... Or just plain bad. It now becomes an "issue" to be clarified and discussed. Decisions put off. Timeliness is ignored.

A teacher has to bring Johnny's problem to his Principal as an issue.

On paper a problem is not judgmental....while protecting the feelings of Johnny. Feelings are now more important than facts.

I don't take issue with swimsuits.

Issues can be discussed over a period of time before the politically correct response is crafted.

I don't disagree. I am not allowed to disagree. I am allowed to bring up an issue. LOL.

Most all of learning from the beginnings of time came from trial and error. It all came the moment something went wrong. Or when pain was felt. One doesn't learn if punishment is not real or put off.

Rules and regulations are in place to protect and encourage, not confuse.

Can you imagine, (probably not because you ain't been there), a US Marine Corps recruit telling his Drill Instructor that he has an "issue" with the amount of pushups he has to do? Bet they were immediately doubled without discussion. There is no issue when life and death is at stake. Training must be tough or learning withers.

There are many good rules and good values that must be protected on the spot. The same goes for the child and parent… and student and teacher. A "NO" must be immediate and meaningful. Again… I argue take the cell phone away. That is not an issue. That is the new punishment. Then spank…LOL.

I don't take issue with swimsuits. There are more important things to address.

I take issue with our lack of leadership in education and government.

The lack of values leadership.

The lack of moral leadership.

The lack of cultural leadership.

I take issue with waste and overspending at home and in government.

I take issue with bureaucracy.

I take issue with our abandonment of where we came from.

I take issue with our abandonment of God.

Is that issue enough?

One Nation

One nation with liberty and justice for all.

That is who we are. Or who we said we would be.

Is there still a flag we pledge allegiance to?

Schools in all their wisdom have abandoned the "Pledge of Allegiance"... Because?? Because it fosters right wing thinking... Aka patriotism??

Are we nuts? Hello millennials? You are sowing the seeds of self-destruction.

We had better backpedal fast or we will not have the spine to face the evil headed our way. Real evil, real murder, real disrespect for human beings, mutilation of everything.

What do we love?? Cell phones sharing feelings? Is there not anything to love worth protecting?

Should there at least be a pledge of allegiance to Truth... or Love?? Recited before the first class of every day?

Or the pledge of allegiance to feelings.... Everyone to their own first, then others??

One nation with liberty and justice for all.

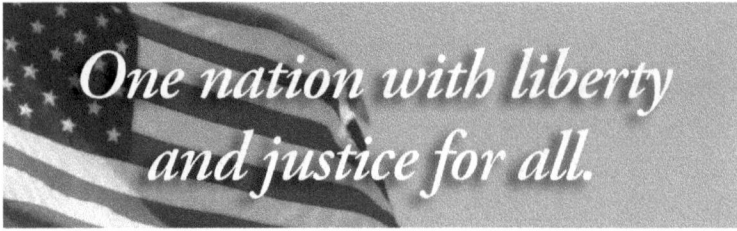

Don't we believe in anything? Is there not something about values and what is right and good to pledge an allegiance to???

Our flag represents the values of our nation and all the brave men and women who have died for its principles. Our military made up mostly of our young comes together under tight rules. Rules to protect them and to make them stronger. They believe in something. To protect their nation and Flag. Thank God…

I say no more pandering to feelings. Our teachers and parents know what is right down deep. Political correctness is not right. It should be labelled and mocked for it protects only the bureaucrat.

Let's pledge ourselves to something rather than nothing.

Written a long time ago, and in our schools until recently…

"I pledge allegiance to the Flag of the United States of America, and to the Republic for which it stands, **one nation under God**, indivisible, with liberty and justice for all."

The Orchestra

Wonder how so many people can play so many different instruments at the same time and it sounds like music?

Just this morning there were kids, middle school, high school, college, and adult musicians… maybe 100 of them all producing coherent and beautiful music. It's not like a rock band where everybody solos while trying to sing the song. Admittedly, some are great and we are lucky to have Adele's unique gift.

But this wacko, this come-together orchestra nailed it. How can so many different people ever come together and produce this moment of art?

Breathtaking. I even cupped my ears to make sure I was missing nothing.

Ok… they did have a conductor standing on a podium so he could easily be seen by all. His music sheets appeared more complex than the musicians and his baton floated and jabbed unifying all the different instruments.

Each musician was a specialist in their beloved instrument. To be even this good they had to love it. A lifetime of hours spent

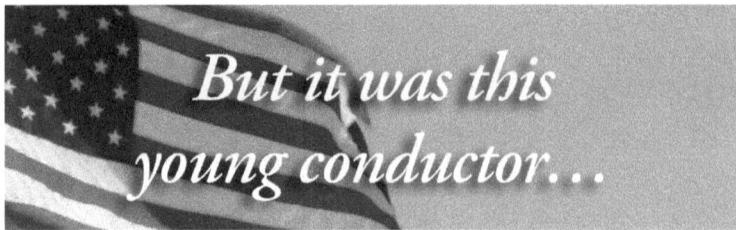

playing so it became reflexive. You gotta love it to practice so much. Love has to be at the center of it. Love has to be at the center of anything that is good, of anything that is excellent.

But it was this young conductor, gifted with a genuineness that each musician responded to. Eyes always checking back to. For the good of all they allowed themselves to be conducted. Wow! They believed.

Today's world is dysfunctional in too many arenas. No one is allowing anyone to tell them what to do.

Minority opinions rule.

Feelings rule.

Emotional chaos.

Internet driven information overabundance is stifling too many minds. Science marches on to its own baton... That's okay.

Media today is without guidance other that satiating the need for romance and murder. Both rammed into our brains teaching us nothing other than the next episode is next week. Viewership. Profits.

I want a conductor to help me make good music. I want to be

someone that matters. I want, as we all do, to make a difference...
And the right kind. I want to help other's lives be better. I want to
be a mini-conductor for good.

I want to be a part of the great orchestra.

And I want the choir to be angels.

Their Conductor is supposedly the best.

Love At First Sight

Cupid is an angel?

What does the head of a baby look like as it emerges from the womb into its first light and breath?

The tears of pain from the mother's cheeks fall on this head.

It is love at first sight.

She is the first to love her child.

The bond to the mother is hereby cemented into eternity.

"Where is my mommy?" is a primordial cry since time began. And still remains hidden today in the pain of the living, of the lost, the lonely... This cry remains hidden deep within for life. Grownups don't want to admit it....

A mother could have been lacking or lost in the abandonments of life. Even then... someday she will be understood, loved more, and even forgiven, and loved even more.

We do not choose our mothers. Cupid does.

If life is tough or we go down the selfish road, love becomes the only thing we trust or are drawn to. The emotions of love are so

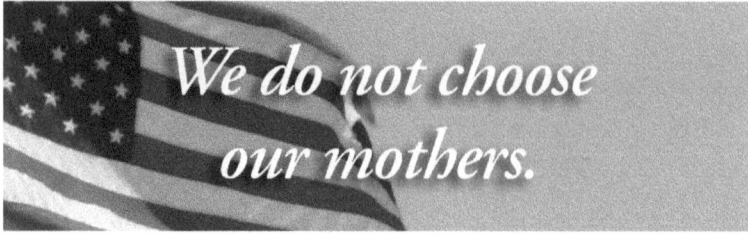

We do not choose our mothers.

magically compelling and transcend all logic. In the attraction phase we totally yield to feelings, both heartfelt and physical. Holding hands as if there were not a care in the world. If blessed, holding hands at death.

We can give birth to all kinds of goodness. We can hold hands and guide others. Their love will be felt in our private pride. Knowing you helped is knowing you loved. You don't have to sleep with or marry every person you love.

Looking across a room you can feel drawn to a beautiful woman or a strong man.

It is so exciting to feel love at first sight… even if it is only for a night?

No, the love we are talking about is deeper, more substantive.

You will give up your life for your child.

I would.

Would you send your Son to die?

Someone did.

T-Ruth

T-REX was a pretty scary monster.

When you are scared it is easier for evil to win.

Church is scary to many.

Evil gets to win.

I have heard 1,000's of sermons from 100's of pulpits.

I can say that maybe a dozen preachers were great, significant, and moving.

Because we want the Truth.

We want the Truth about love.

We want to know the Truth about His Love.

The Story of Ruth is a story of Love.

In Cape Porpoise, Maine we have a Ruth.

She tells the Truth exquisitely.

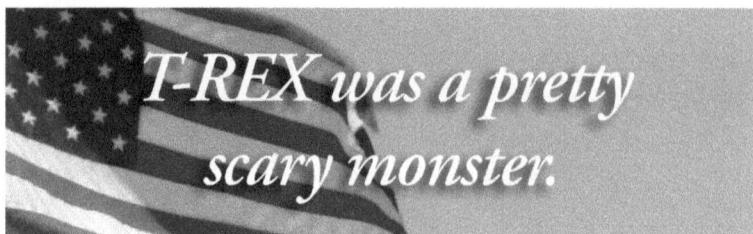

T-REX was a pretty scary monster.

I love her.

T-Ruth.

I Love Lucy

I loved Lucy and Desi.

They argued a lot.

He was Cuban and Lucy was this hilarious redhead who could not stop making things complicated and funny.

It was black and white TV.

It was everyone's first real comedy and a family drama.

We all got to laugh. At Lucy and at Desi… and life… The comedy that is in everyday life was brought to us. It was all clean, no parental guidance required. LOL.

There was no need for ratings way back then… No blood. Violence was underplayed. Frowned upon.

They still have reruns today so you can see what life was like before we started to make trash permissible. Today's TV is akin to a trash compactor.

Lucy had strong ideas of what was right and wrong. We agreed and laughed. Desi was the foil… We men all sided with him in spite of his wonderful accent. LOL.

I loved Lucy and Desi.

Actually this show may have been our first introduction to immigration and how good it could be… Immigrate and the process worked. The bureaucracy was still manageable. Immigrants could feel like people, not abused statistics. Multicultural marriage was made acceptable. We learned to root for it. Maybe this show was the harbinger of mixed marriage?

So how did a nutty comedy with a nutty couple so endear itself to us? Was it just honest? It played on the natural comedy of husband and wife, not shock and sensationalism. No borderline language. It said a family could disagree and still function.

"Whatever" was never disrespectfully heard.

Smartphones were science fiction.

Life was good.

I Love Lucy.

Flying Fortress

It was called the B-17 and then the Flying Fortress.

Built before most of us were born.

Evil existed in Europe and the Pacific. It took years of heavy bombing to stop the advance of this evil. It is a shame that it couldn't be stopped earlier. But debate, conferences, and delay gave it all the time it needed to reach critical mass. It even required nuclear weapons to stop it in the Pacific.

Evil has to be nipped in the beginning. The earlier the easier. Except that takes judgement. Who is going to judge…? aka… be judgmental?? A taboo word. Hmmm…

Maybe we need a Family Fortress that will bomb ignorance and political correctness. A husband and wife sticking it out while they control the teaching of values, good and bad in a positive way to their children. It takes rules…and punishment… where morals are taught and respected. Where humility and compassion frame the learning. If selfishness or evil starts it is love bombed immediately. Tough love and whatever else is required.

Kids have to be taught to enjoy and respect work. Those raised

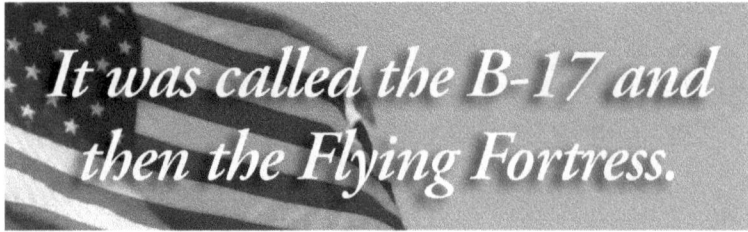

on farms have a better chance as the parents have more control. Especially if the driveway is a mile long… LOL. Family Fortress.

If parents weren't raised in the same ethic, then all this is folly.

Where does a parent go to learn how to build their Family Fortress?

There have to be other Family Fortresses that were built successfully?

Search them out.

I am told many are in the hangar with the Steeple on top.

Heavens To Betsy

"Heavens to Betsy" is probably no longer said.

It meant you were surprised at something…

Today I would imagine the replacements have a lot of swear words.

Maybe Betsy was a curious girl and when she looked up into the heavens at night she created her phrase, "Heavens to Betsy". The stars and planets became hers in the blackness. Not afraid to keep looking up. Actually, finding it impossible to take her eyes off all this beauty, she became entranced. She fell in love with the incomprehensible complexity of a message being sent from infinite light years away.

Stars that were in existence before our planet Earth and her solar system were formed. Profoundly disturbing and worthy of worship. Ask the Mayans in Mexico. And the numerous other cultures 1,000's of years ago.

All these stars just make no sense. Maybe only to lovers in the still of their moments. Hands held in amazement of the beauty above. Like love being sent to us. Hmmm?

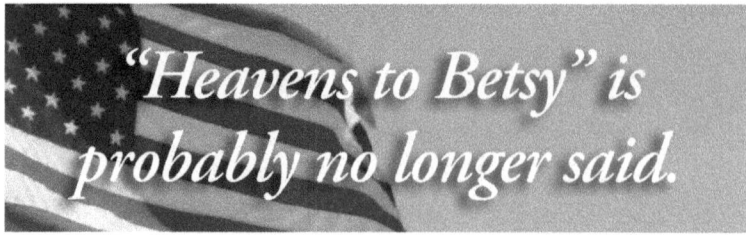

Now there are black holes into which matter is absorbed and lost?? Sure makes no sense.

And each year as the telescopic lenses keep improving… and even from orbit. And even from spacecraft sent to our farthest planets no end is found. New galaxies behind old galaxies. And we thought we knew everything?? LOL. Where does it end? I think we will have to come to the conclusion that it doesn't.

So these infinite galaxies, trillions of light years away, were always there? What is always?? Big Bang??? Oh give me a break. That created it? Stupid theory.

There is no answer but One.

Complex logic is not required.

Only Faith.

Something had to be created by some Creator.

If that is accepted in Faith, then all makes sense.

It is that simple.

"Heavens to Betsy".

Headless Horseman

He has been riding since the middle ages.

The simple image of headlessness has frightened all continents and is even American folklore.

When you were a kid and you first read this story you tasted fear.

In the Middle East heads are being severed for amusement and messaging.

We are nothing without our head. The miracle of our brain and our uniqueness is centered there. Brain damage and you no longer are the person you were. Why is the skull so hard? Like the best of crash helmets. Protecting our control and identity center.

Simply put, without a head you are dead.

We all know that some people are crazy, or at least seem so to us. Differing opinions can make us think the other is crazy. Like really… without a head.

Some people are selfish and evil. They have no moral sense. They are lost in themselves and metaphorically are acting as if they had no head.

He has been riding since the middle ages.

When a head of state is deposed and a nation has no leader or no head, will the replacement be any better?

We all think we are the jockey of our life and are pointing our horse in the right direction. Yet our odds of winning diminish with every bad choice, with every selfish act. We whip our horse to go faster, but he can only go so fast for so long.

In the bleachers the women are all wearing their fancy hats cheering us on. They want winners.

But the horseman is headless until he takes a position in the gate of caring about others and puts his heart in his head.

Now he can win.

As he jumps from his new Pearly starting gate..........

Love of Life

We all sure love life.

And we all sure love it when there is no pain.

And we all sure love it when we are laughing.

And we all sure love it when we are loving.

There so many exciting things to do in life. Isn't life a crazy concoction? We get to do most whatever we want... At least when governments are fair and free and not causing poverty.

For the most blessed of us we get to travel, eat, play, celebrate and enjoy the amenities of modern life. Pizza and TV. Without fear. Without fear.

Beauty unspoiled is still accessible to us. The Rockies, the coasts, the wildernesses, the cultures.....

We love life, we love it. We love freedom, we love it.

We love being protected.

We love being loved.

Our good fortune blinds us to the love that the majority on

We love being loved.

our planet never sees. Repressive cultures.... Poverties beyond imagination. Abuses beyond all understanding. Women and children being raped. Nothing said. Too difficult to change conditions or cultures. Hey, radical abuse is going on in many more countries than ever admitted.

So we get to go on loving life. And we deserve it... do we? Are we born to circumstance beyond our say??

We get to taste love and freedom.

What is it like if you never get anything other than a glimpse of an outside world on TV... All looking like science fiction... And so classy like "Real Wives Of Beverly Hills"?

There always has been a war between love and hate.

Good and evil.

Fairness and unfairness.

Compassion and indifference.

Generosity and greed.

Giving and taking.

We know the list never ends...

It all boils down to…

A Love of Life…

Or…

A Life of Love.

Forever After

What in the world do they mean by "forever after"???

Does it imply that once something is done it is forever a part of history, ours and the world's?

Never forgotten.

But maybe forgiven?

When people die where do they go? Into the "forever after"??

Ok… sounds like a big stadium or something…. Doesn't seem too cool. Giving all of one's life so we can go somewhere vague, if we even go anywhere? Maybe we just die and stop being. Doesn't seem right for my mom and dad who were really great parents. I put them through the ringer. They have to be somewhere rather than nowhere. They loved me. I learned about love and rules and fairness. They put me in good schools. I love them more than ever now that I understand life a little better. I will love them forever… or as long as I can.

It is so nice to have pictures of them I have blown up on canvas. And also put on our digital photo frames. A slide show of life with even a motion sensor to turn itself on. Our past is forever playing.

When people die where do they go?

We don't know what the "after" today will bring. We only know the before today...

So this puts life into a confusing configuration. There has to be another way to look at it.

Suppose the "forever after" was some indescribable heaven? That would sure change the ball game and motivation. The only way it can be a factor is for it to be given up to Faith. To have a Faith. To believe in something. To believe in God. Yes, it takes a leap of faith... so what? Then the meaning of life has some purpose. We can examine good and bad. We can make something of our life.

For without faith there is nothing.

Faith compels one to think.

To do what gives the most meaning to the moment.

I prefer to believe I will see my mom and dad again.

To share our journeys.

To Love in the "Forever After"... forever.

Civil War

Let's keep it civil unless it is about race.

Our Civil War in the late 1,800's saw Americans fighting and killing fellow Americans. 600,000 of them.

It was nasty and up close. It was not civil. It was about ending slavery. Allowing color to no longer be denied the freedom to love freedom.

When you fight a war there is nothing civil about it. Innocent people and children get slaughtered. You have to see it to believe it. You know what is right and wrong in your gut, not on the internet or TV.

The war in the Middle East is disgusting and repulsive and against everything we have ever fought for. The solution will not be civil. And it must come soon, very soon.

Families in our country are in their own civil war as the seductions of substance, sensuality, materialism, and deceit are running rampant. There is no way a parent can discipline their child to save them that is politically correct. Creative punishment,

Let's keep it civil unless it is about race.

including corporal, must be part of the mix. Take away cell phones for a day???

The family is at war with itself. He loves this, she loves that… and that is the way it is. Texting is a god. Freedom to do anything is the new god. Established values are mocked.

This is war. Can we keep it civil?

What about the war going on inside us every day? Where we have to make decisions and choices that are good and bad. Do we reflect enough?? Or go with the easier or more sensual choice?

Is 100% honesty who you are? Or should be?

Is 100% integrity your goal?

Who are the people you feel comfortable around? Or think are good? Are they really? How can we judge if we aren't honest? Evil and temptation are everywhere.

Who would we like to be? Who can be used as a model? It is so tempting to steal from our future to enjoy the present… Husbands and wives know what civil war is as they try to serve their family. Arguments are often not civil….

Love is in peril.

Love is in peril if we don't recognize evil.

I wish we could drop a bomb on evil.

It would not be civil.

But is not good worth dying for?

Assisted Living

Leave me alone, I can do it on my own.

I can climb Mt. Everest if I want or run 26 miles if I want.

Or drink or smoke if I want.

If I want. If I want.

One soon learns that we need a guide or a trainer to show us how to do it better. When we are young so many things seem possible and they fill dreams with smiles.

However, the older we get we see that there are people older who know more. Our new assistance providers.

How do we know if we know enough about love??

To whom do we turn for advice?

Some go to a tanning booth to be more loveable… What one wears to attract takes time and instruction if we really want to "look" appealing. For guys our car suffices if it is cool. LOL.

When we get really old we are often parked in an assisted living facility. They all have these lovely names to infer peace and

Leave me alone, I can do it on my own.

contentment for the residents/patients… One can just write a monthly check and grandpa is in assisted living. All his needs tended to. Except that, for the most part, they aren't. No longer with family. And they seldom visit… And the attendants and nurses are always changing. Our needs go unheard. A parking lot for love memories.

Without compassionate leadership the atmosphere is stifling. One withdraws into silence. Or the droning of the television. No one knows what the wait for bathing and cleaning is like…. Erratic and unpleasant. Bed sores indicating unacceptable follow-up. Bureaucratic needs trumping love. Paperwork corrected first. The paperwork comes before the patient. Bed sores can wait.

Assisted living without love. The quiet private pain deep in the soul of the lonely still living...

In Latin countries and Europe, a family stays together. Grandpa is at his home with his family. Seems nicer.

We all need assistance in living from the first breath.

The best assistance comes from those whose heart is in the right place. Feeling the love sores of others.

Love givers.

Holding us close.

Assisted loving.

Try Sunday morning.

Love In Love Out

Before computers we really didn't know "garbage in garbage out".

The dawning of the digital era meant you became a bit supplier.

1's and 0's became the yes and no of all decisions.

Entries into a computer have to be correct or nothing happens. They are the order of our new life. Storing all the knowledge of man in tiny bits. Calculating orbital trajectories to the analyzing of cancer cells. A little bit too much?? LOL.

Everything has to be correct. Every input has to be correct for any kind of correct answer to come out. And wow, look at all we have today that is digital! Amazing. Overwhelming numbers of 1's and 0's everywhere. And even on spacecraft heading to the outer reaches of our galaxy.

Garbage in garbage out. One incorrect digit can disable an enormous program!

Is there a parallel to our living? A parable???

Again we have to consider good and bad. Like two bits. One can destroy the other? Every selfish decision is garbage in. How do

Garbage in garbage out.

we learn to identify them? Maybe checking in with our heart and its feeling of conscience.

Do we have a conscience?

Do we have anything deep down inside that signals comfort or discomfort?

How do we learn to listen?

Too much garbage in and we can't hear our heart.

Greed, sin, dishonesty, substance abuse…. All forms of abuse render your computer dysfunctional. We are dysfunctional and we can't see that we are. But… if we had been following the Rules, we would know it and we would feel good and right.

Maybe praying for insight and direction? Oops! Praying is a "no-no" word. OK, but we need to know the Truth before we can make a decision.

It takes a lot of "good" love to heal one.

The right kind of Love can purify what we put in.

Then what comes out is the real us.

And we know it.

And we produce more good love.

And everybody feels a little "bit" better.

Love in Love out.

Love Pains

"Ouch... that hurt!"

Hey, what's a little sting?

A bee sting is not that bad unless you have an allergy.

Wasps are a little worse, but you will get over it.

Now... the love bug...??? That is a real bite....

As kids we love our mom first, then our dad if he is a good guy... but, if not, we will love him anyway.

We always look to our parents for approval, and affirmation, and love. Good families with good values, good rules, good fairness, good discipline, and good humilities end up doing good, real good. Good love.

But if any of the above ain't there "we got a problem Houston". Think of families where the dad has left. Having no dad is real sad. Was a mom meant to be a dad? I don't think so. Your call.

If values are inconsistent, then the kid has all the ammunition to be an attitude machine. Same goes for all the rest of us. No

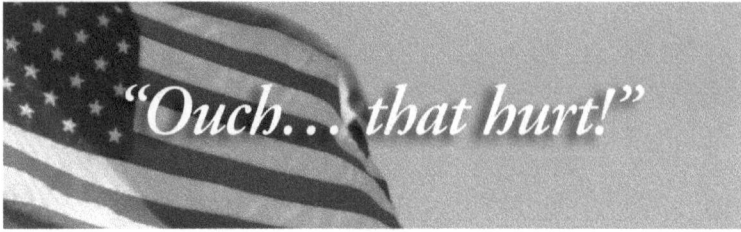

"Ouch... that hurt!"

discipline, no tough rules, no "NO's" and you get the attitude machine and its cell phone army.

The kid hides his serious love pains behind his infinite insecurities as does the adult who didn't have the strong foundation. The cycle of indifference to real values must be broken. Generations of neglect must be addressed. Now. Just do it. Now.

Love pains.... Generations of them.

Now what is also bad is when your girlfriend says she does not love you any more. You gotta be stupid not to see it coming. But remember the old expression?? "Love blinds"?

No, not on the windows stupid, in your head.

We drink and drug the pain of loneliness away. Loneliness means without love.

You been there?

Love also hurts at birth. Our own Betsy is so big I don't know how she can possibly deliver the new boy. But she will, and the pains of love at birth will be borne and celebrated. Amazing.

If aborted, the child will never know love pain.

The mother will always know its name in her heart... Forever.

I bet we all would like to chime in on this subject.

No one has ever not experienced a love pain.

Once upon a time it really hurt upon a Cross.

Fight Right

A friend suggested I write on "celebrate life".

I can't.

The world is in chaos.

Brutality is being re-invented as acceptable in the minds of young praying males in the Middle East.

Storm clouds of chanting. Children brainwashed to see our celebrations as selfish and evil. The United States of America is their great Satan. How can we combat this? What tools and weapons do we use?

Our children are no longer being taught history, values, or what is Evil. Many are just cell phone celebrating their hours and weeks and months away. Being conditioned to ignore the obvious.

Yes, goodness and caring for others is enacted by many of us for those who have less. These are moments of celebration. The best feeling in life is putting a smile on the face of someone who has lost hope. Faith breeds hope.

The eyes of the poor and put-aside have empty tear ducts.

Nothing to celebrate.

I will celebrate when our country finds unity and resolve. A coming together to face Evil head on… heads on… not off. We are debating and discussing the Evil across the oceans. Blinding ourselves to the weakness we have created. Our knapsacks are filled with entertainment providers. Look the other way and party on.

The toughest war we have ever faced is at our doorstep. I fear it will need the commitment we showed in WWII. And we are not capable of it.

There is a next 9/11 ahead of us.

Don't you feel the draft?

Maybe we need one again.

We can celebrate when we win.

It is right to fight.

Final Choice

Who do we want to be?

When we are young we look up to celebrities and sports heroes…
OK, even Navy SEALs.

We want to be somebody.

Deep inside we want to be somebody.

Which is what we are but don't know it.

We can make all kinds of choices and learn that most of them end
up hurting.

When we reach middle age we have responsibilities and families,
hopefully. Keeping families whole and together is a challenge.
Never more so than today.

We learn about love from parents and family. They create the lens
through which we discern in what direction we wish to go. How
much money to make. How much love to give and to whom… or
to what.

We are constantly observing others to see how happy they are.

Who do we want to be?

We want more love. As much as we can get. Real love, not bought love.

When we get older we can see the mistakes we made and keep hidden. Keeping them hidden requires energy. Keeping too many things hidden means you are broken and not free from guilt and are looking over your shoulder.

Life is all about our quest for love.

We have to do things we may not love…like most jobs… But wouldn't it be fantastic if we could do something productive that we love? We would be happier and could then love more.

When we finally learn to love loving others by helping them, we will have made the 'rightest feeling decision' of our life.

When this becomes our final choice then we have grown up.

In your old age you can carry a smile you have dreamed of. Without attachments.

Our smile. Humble, but knowing.

Knowing our uniqueness has been always there but not perfectly formed.

For only Love can take every uniqueness and shape its potential and final glory.

The choice is ours, finally.

For He so loved the world…

Genuine Leather 2

How do you know if it is genuine or not?

If something is stamped "Genuine Leather" how do you know for sure?

Isn't there a government agency that oversees everything labelled "genuine"??

My wallet is stamped "Genuine Leather" and really must be as after 5 years it has only become better. Molding its shape to whatever is inside. But is so smooth and still looking like new. Stitching as good as day purchased.

It takes time to find out if something is genuine... And when it is, it must be cherished and protected.

Of course, you know what this is leading up to?

"Genuine Love" is stamped on the minds of all at a wedding. All our lives we search for true love. The first time we feel it we want it to go on forever...and believe it will. That is just who we are on this planet. Maybe it will be different on Mars. LOL.

Where does this first feeling of love come from..?? It feels like

How do you know if it is genuine or not?

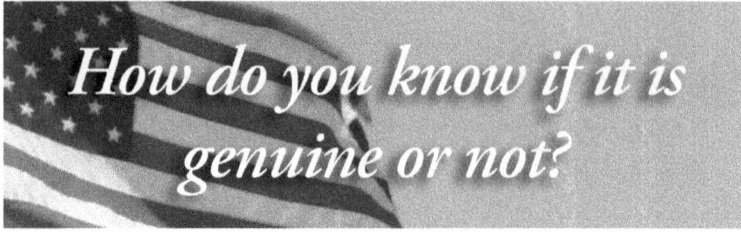

it starts in the heart. In fact, for most of us, when we follow our heart we feel more comfortable. If the heart is ignored we become lost and live destructive lifestyles of substances, things, or self. There is no hope for genuine love until after one reaches bottom. A nasty place to go. But once there and they look up..... Genuine love will forgive and repair and bless.

Society today is not interested in genuineness, just convenience.

Genuine friendships must stand the test of time and cannot be found on the cell phone or internet. In fact, genuine danger lurks on the internet waiting to sever our contact with our heart.

Our first genuine love came from our mother. And boy did it feel good even though we weren't aware. We all want to go back to those simpler times when we were shrouded in love and innocence.

I just pulled my wallet out and looked at how perfect it is. Been in my back pocket every day for years. Now that is punishment... LOL. Genuine for sure.

If we want genuine we must search out right from wrong. Choose good over evil. Choose others over self.

Genuinize your smile.

Be genuine.

Love everybody.

From your heart.

He did.

EVOL

How could I be writing about love and not see this?

4 letters that are at the heart of life.

At the center of everything that happens that is good and bad.

When love gets upside down. When love goes backwards. Or reversed you get EVOL. Crazy? Right?

Every human being wants to be loved. We hide this need every way possible. As if it were a negative...? Why? When we experience the feelings and unselfish sensation of love we give in. We love it. Willing to commit our whole self to a forever love.

Your first love? Couldn't wait to see each other. Time stands still. The heart resonates in the Truth of Love. We would give up our life gladly for love. A girl's eyes searching her man's for strength and security. The poetry of love. Hey, how many love poems are there? Books? Songs? Movies?

Love sells.

We can't get enough of it.

Fortunes are made on love.

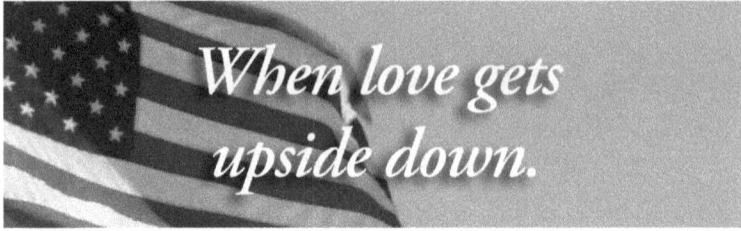

When love gets upside down.

But so is misfortune.

Keeping a love pure, and protecting it, means a commitment to Truth and honesty and unselfishness. It can be done. It ain't easy. And you can never quit. Or you invalidate all you have strived to gain. Love brings peace if you are up to it.

But if love is selfish then it is not love. Hearts and innocence are devastated when love is abused or used.

Helping others is love. It is not about self-gratification. It is good. It is who we were meant to be. We look up to those who serve others unselfishly.

Love backwards is our challenge.

If we replace the "O" with an "I" you see what we get.

It is vicious and brutal and ever-present.

EVIL.

Love Song

My first love song was sung by my mother…" Rock a Bye Baby on the treetop…"

These days I have been listening to a lot of love music via small Bluetooth speakers when working on paperwork.

I have made two playlists: Love Hurts and Latin Love.

You know…"All You Need Is Love", Anything Adele, "You Make Loving Fun", "Need You Now", "Easy Lover", "Hot Stuff", "Over The Rainbow"….and on and on and on. We all have our favorite love songs that immediately reach into us when they start. What fun it is to create love compilations.

I also created a list called Latin Love. I love to play it when I am working with our Hispanic staff. I had them each give me 3 of their favorite songs. I did the iTunes Store download, $1.29 each. Now I play it even when I work out. Their love songs are better than ours! Melodic and crazy beautiful… and much more romantic! I don't know what they are saying, but it doesn't matter.

Love songs are in every country, in every language.

In some countries they are considered dangerous and are screened

Love songs are in every country, in every language.

by dark government agencies… Very sad… hope is diminished. Futures diminished.

Concert music and songs always talk about love, and the hurt that comes when it is not fulfilled. So many themes. Love song lyrics yearn for the truth in love more than sermons in churches. Our young and our old take refuge in them.

Parties of all sorts in all kinds of locations blast out love themes. The lyrics are the poetry of the masses. We will not give them up. They bring hope, comfort, and excitement. And we get to keep them forever.

Can you remember it started with vinyl records, then 8-Track tapes, then cassettes, then CDs, then iPod, iPhone, Bluetooth, and now back to vinyl.

We have to keep our love songs close to play when we need them.

They are a kind of reassurance that love is important.

That life without love is meaningless.

We play them in our store.

I wonder what Love Song they play in an abortion clinic?

Extortion 17

Love takes so many shapes and circumstances.

Puppies are the best… nope, kids are, until they do wrong.

How do we love them out of their predicaments?

Here in the USA we have most all the freedom we need to make sure love finds an answer. Love that is easy and love that is tough. In our country and most western cultures love is free to be… There are some rules and regulations, but nothing like the Middle-East and Asia.

On August 6, 2011 a Chinook helicopter was shot down, maybe ambushed by Taliban, in the mountains of Afghanistan. 38 lives were lost, 15 from SEAL Team 6. They were already in landing mode. The code name of the chinook was Extortion 17.

What's love got to do with it? Ask the mothers and fathers.

The Middle-East is a crazy world that is trying to destroy our freedom, our education, our nation, and our love. Young men in the military get it. We often don't.

We love "love". What price are we willing to pay for it?

Love that is easy and love that is tough.

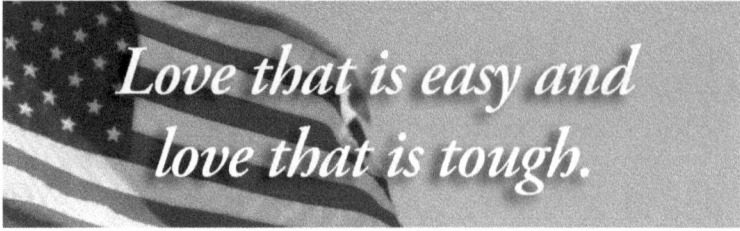

Without the rule of law we have chaos. Without love we have chaos. Love is good and can do more good than anything else… when not corrupted.

These men who died were great lovers. Great lovers of freedom, justice, and good. Mike Monsoor, Michael Murphy, and so many others sacrificed themselves for the love of a brother teammate. Google their stories. What about all the guys who come back with PTSD after seeing things that no one should see?

They see what a total lack of love can do.

They see Evil.

We send lovers in harm's way.

Will they ever be able to love again?

Blue Angels

They fell in love with flying.

All men have at one time considered flying.

Stinson, Piper Cub, DC3, P40, P51, F100, F16, F117, B2, Mercury, Gemini, Apollo and so many more.

Those who do will never forget the sunrises, sunsets, and missions.

The Blue Angels show us what an art form flying is. The poets of the clouds??

It is another form of love… in the heavens… or in orbit…. or on the moon. Have you seen that photo of earth taken on the moon? Beauty everywhere… even on the desolate surfaces of our solar system's planets… where man's love has not yet left a footprint.

I have been in the emergency room of our hospital today. He is 96 and never flew. My wife's dad. He will be flying soon.

In and out came the blue angels. Everyone in the ER is dressed in full blue…a great dark royal blue kinda. They don't have to change them as often.

All men have at one time considered flying.

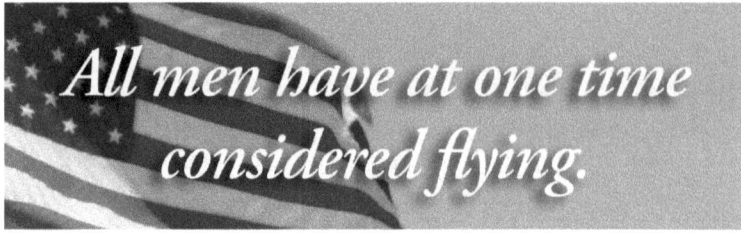

I asked this blue angel where the glamour was. She said there was none. Just that her work had to be done. It needed her. Day after day. And she never sees daylight or clouds until she goes home. They have to get real tired by the end of the day…. If not on night duty. Bet she sleeps like an angel.

These are jobs serving the injured and sick. Life and death are part of the daily mosaic. There is a symphony of quality caring in our Naples Community Hospital.

The young doctor was focused, yet alive with personality. Not corporate. Nice.

One can choose any profession. But only if you love it will it love you back. You can only grow "in" love.

Without love you run out of oxygen.

This oxygen is made when you are helping others.

We call it Love.

Loqua City

They talk a lot in Loqua City.

People come and people go.

They have much more to talk about than before they came.

Everyone loves to come here to hear the latest and obtain a convincing understanding of the newest trivia. Serious matters are not as important. Celebrities and politicians and news people are the exception.

To speak convincingly we have to believe that what we are saying is true. Truth is powerful. Finding out what it really is takes effort and a good amount of research to be sure. Half-truths are just that and get us nowhere other than words of little meaning. Our reputation also suffers if we only have bits of Truth.

If we talk too much, too often… a label gets affixed to us. Future opinions are dismissed. We are branded as someone to avoid when truth is being sought.

Some people really speak from their heart…and it rings true to them and to us. We want to hear more from these people.

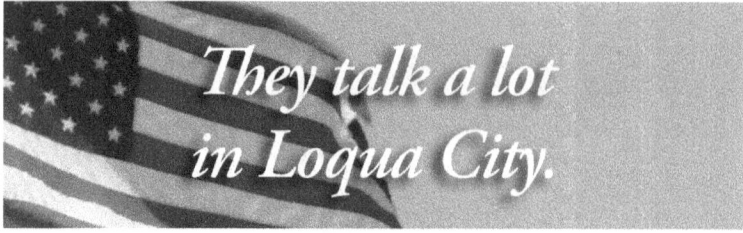
They talk a lot in Loqua City.

We have to love truth to be important to anyone.

There is so much partial and biased thinking that makes it hard to find the truth. So much nonsense clutters our path to Truth. Talk, Talk, Talk, Talk. Everyone seems to like to hear their own voice. That is what loquacious means. Loquacity in Loqua City. That's where all the talkers are from or headed to. Great place to retire to and talk your head off.

Of course there are motivational speakers and all kinds of people gifted at public speaking. But a good portion of it is just emotional fluff with truth and reality missing.

The only words that have real meaning have to do with helping someone. If we truly are trying …then there is that ring of truth again.

You don't have to be loquacious to get your point across, just sincere and from your heart.

The brain is great, but the heart trumps it. Many fear truth because it dismantles their façade. A façade they will do anything to protect.

Love is Truth. If you love helping others, then you are living in the Truth of life. For they are synonymous…. Love and Truth.

Often it takes few words. Maybe just a yes or a no.

Our hearts know Love.

Our hearts know the Truth.

"Love one another as I have loved you."

Lucy In The Sky

She too had to die.

She was so beautiful and young.

And to the end.

She had to die.

At home.

Just didn't wake up.

No pain.

Hard to know really how she saw things and life. She was born in the woods, almost like a manger. Couldn't pick her up for a while. In a wire enclosure in the woods.

God, did she turn out perfect. Love eyes. Crazy black rimmed love eyes. Like she was made of gold she was so perfect for us. Could have won awards but she didn't have to go that route. Every day she won our award. And when you petted her, both of you were somewhere else. The perfect retriever.

Wouldn't it be wonderful when we die we find out that all the

She was so beautiful and young.

stars in all the galaxies were really lights from those who loved and now are gone? Can we say heavens?? LOL.

Okay, that's silly I admit. But why are there so many stars that we can't even begin to see yet beyond the farthest galaxy which will have galaxies beyond it.

The hell with it... what's wrong with "Love Lights"?? Diamonds of past love... all sending us the wonders of love to wonder about. LOL?

Okay again, we can be scientific and do a spectrum analysis of these lights. Are they reflections like diamonds?? How can one ever get to them to find out?

I guess we are all free to love as we wish and to see love as we wish.

It doesn't matter.

Our Lucy is in the sky with diamonds.

Farther Father

How far away does a father have to be to not be a father?

How far away does a mother have to be to not be a mother?

So many children are left alone to answer this question.

Growing up without their love.

Hidden cries of rejection mold and form the new child lost.

The "want" to be loved never leaves….and is now more hidden.

They say love conquers all. Never give up on love because love alone can heal and nourish the injured, the abandoned… nothing else. It is hard for them to trust love. Mistakes are made. They hurt. These go into the hiding place too.

Parents get injured by denying their child the love that they wished to give… but chose otherwise.

Love is at the center of it all for every human, however in denial they may be. Life can only be ennobled by not giving up on love. Loving even when we are not loved back.

When the child forgives the parent they can love again.

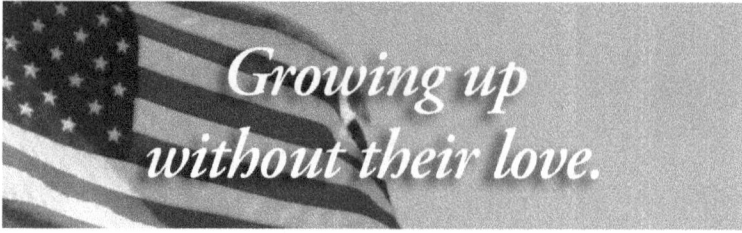

Forgiveness is the path back to love. Forgiveness celebrates creation.

Marriages fail.

Love never does.

The greatest antibiotic is love.

The greatest pain killer is love.

On the Cross was forgiveness and love.

From the Bottom of My Heart

How deep **IS** the bottom of a heart?

What kind of dive gear do you need to get to the bottom?

Are there wrecks of all kinds there?

Kinda like we sank some ships along the way.

Things we did that we wish we hadn't.

Things that can make us feel uncomfortable.

When one says "From the bottom of my heart" we are trying to gain trust and are saying that we are telling the truth. "From the bottom of my heart"…yep…

Is it not saying that our heart is really at the center of us? Why does one use this expression? Is there anything else one could say that is better?

"Trust me"? "Believe me"? "The Gospel truth"?

Nope… "From the bottom of my heart" seems to be the winner.

How deep is the bottom of a heart?

Maybe we should be saying it more often? There are some people who do not have to say it as they have made a reputation for telling the truth. We look up to people who tell the truth. Some of us go to churches to find out about other kinds of truth. Maybe we don't find it there, or maybe we do…?

Our heart is where our love comes from. We can feel things in our heart. Emotions. Powerful emotions. Powerful beliefs. Amazing. Why is this organ the center of everything? We go **TO** it for truth. We go to it for the validation of love.

I think we all want to love more. Sure there is the love of things and activities. But we most of all we want our heart to feel good.

It will…

If we can learn to love the Truth.

If we can learn to help others all the time.

Then our life can become all it has the potential to be.

I am telling you this from the bottom of my heart.

First Place

Remember when we were kids and one of our classmates got First Place in something?

It seemed so important.

Or a Gold Medal in the Olympics!

First Place people always get mentioned in the newspaper. And you had something cool to hang on your wall… bedroom or office.

Most of us say we will never get a First Place and not let it bother us. Forgetting that we were First Place in our mother's heart! Birth Certificate?

First Place in the Kentucky Derby, in the Indianapolis 500, or Super Bowl, or Academy Awards… and on and on again. Spelling Bee?

As I am writing this I realized I had a cool First Place. Go guess. Good luck. But it became the fulfillment of a childhood journey. I was a scuba diver at the age of 14 in 1954 in Kentucky…. mostly in lakes and quarries. 10 Years later on my wall here is the class ranking of Class 2-64 at the US Naval School, Underwater Swimmers, US Naval Base, Key West FL. I got First Place. Cool??

The only time in my life so far that a got a First Place. One is enough.

As I have learned more and gotten older I have come to the realization that we can get a First Place every day. Every time I help someone I get a First Place in my heart and the heart of the recipient.

It is so powerful to know you are the winner every time you are unselfish.

I love the feeling.

And I love acting in Love to help someone.

That is what love is all about.

First place is within everybody's reach every day.

Print yourself a certificate.

EPILOGUE

I have been blessed with a journey that has not seen the real poverty or felt the real pain of the majority. Please don't judge me by the immaterial, much less the material. I was born in Bronxville, NY in 1940. Grew up in Louisville and St Louis. Graduated from Yale and went into the Navy. I had the great honor of fulfilling my dream to become a Frogman. I graduated from BUDS Class 31E, Basic Underwater Demolition/Seal School. I was an officer in Underwater Demolition Team 21 which became Seal Team 4 in 1984. I had the honor of recovering several spacecraft, including Gemini 6/7 & AS-201, the very first Apollo Spacecraft to go into space. Wow, did I luck out. Then I spent 40 years in women's retail, in various department stores. Even a year at the World Wrestling Federation... go figure?

I have two great daughters and two grandchildren who have just discovered the water and facemasks. My wife has created probably the #1 women's accessory store in the country as evidenced by how much she is copied. Therein I work and report to her... No comment. LOL.

As you can tell by reading between the lines there is a spiritual side to my journey. Kind of covert as I just want to make a difference unseen.

God Bless You All... Happy Trails.

ACKNOWLEDGEMENTS

I was sure I was done writing…Burned out. Who in the world writes 9 books in 2 years?? Over 500 chapters. Granted chapters are only 2-3 pages long and all the titles make no sense….

But in the middle of the night, just after Christmas 2015, the notion to write about Love popped up. From where? Well, after having written so much about values and life from its funniest to its most serious I realized that Love was inescapably a central ongoing theme. How could there be more to write and not be boring??

But here it is, and I pumped my fist after most chapters. Wow. Chapters really only take 20 minutes to write once the crazy title is put down.

WWIII has already started. We started it by being adrift. Our faces are so glued to our cell phones and social media that we can't look up and see the storm clouds. This book is about love. About making us strong enough to fight for what we deep down care about. A must for all readers, young and not so young. It is often sophisticated and challenging. But the moral bar must be raised if we are to survive.

There are great laughs everywhere within this book and…. in you, if you dare to read it…

Who to thank? Everybody I know. First to mind are all my new friends from No Walls, who have validated values and commitment to what is good. Men learning that there is a war going on against values and all that we stand for. A war where good must rise up and attack evil before it is too late. Who? "Not me!" says the buffoon. Every moment of every day there is an opportunity to be an unseen hero.

Lastly, there are Sandra Simmons-Dawson and Brian Dawson who helped edit and format the books, website, and marketing. Their firm, Money Management Solutions, Inc. dba Customer Finder Marketing http://customerfindermarketing.com/ is a gem.

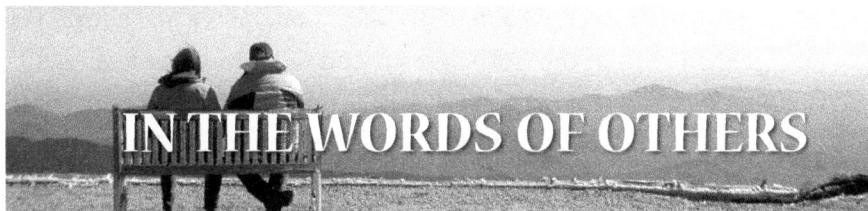

IN THE WORDS OF OTHERS

Reviews for 1-800-Only-For-Love

"One of his best! We learn about love from our parents. Love is the hunger of every human being. Love heals, uplifts, encourages and gives life to those being loved. This book touches on the importance of love the need for it to be shared."

  Dorothy Ederer - Grand Rapids Dominican Catholic Chaplain at Holy Cross Services

"Astounding astute, well stated common sense; an awe-inspiring collection of wisdom that should be consumed by the entire family. I've sent copies to all of my kids."

Commander (SEAL) Tim Hawkins, USN Ret., author, NSW Historian

Reviews for 1-800-I-Am-Unhappy (Volumes 1 and 2)

"This is a book by a man of many directions and passions. Straightforward yet thought provoking. Loyal to his convictions and country. And brave. Sharing. Warrior. Humanitarian."

Jeff Lytle, Editorial Page Editor, Naples Daily News

"As a friend, Chris has helped me understand the inherent conflicts embedded in the language of 'political correctness' and how it attempts, and frequently succeeds, in disguising and defeating the 'truth.' Chris is engaged in a rhetori- cal battle — we need his insight."

William Lord, a 32-year-veteran Executive Producer and Vice-President of ABC News, and Professor of Journalism at Boston University

"Chris writes like he lives. As a man of distinction, he is a voice for the poor, a champion of the truth and a friend of strong character and conviction. His word and his service are a blessing to all who encounter him."

Vann R. Ellison, President/CEO, St. Matthew's House, Inc.

"My nickname for Chris is "Dream-Catcher"- because that's who he is to me. He is my mentor in how to give on His behalf. Freely and generously, Chris offers both words, "God bless you!", and gifts. And all the while he is making a compelling and powerful statement. Chris Bent has discovered a beautiful way to live!"

Rev. Dr. Ruth Merriam, The Church on the Cape (U.M.C.), Cape Porpoise, Maine

"Chris Bent is a very unusual person – Navy SEAL, Yale graduate, successful business owner, and radical Christian who is comfortable talking with anyone at any level in society. He doesn't just talk about faith or caring about the poor, Chris actually lives his faith and he works with the poor. His smile is genuine and reflects his deep joy in life, America, hard work, people and (most definitely) God. I have enjoyed reading his writings; they are different, often hard hitting and sometimes maybe even a little wild. Each one gives a fresh perspective on contemporary lives, reflecting Chris' intel- ligence and faith. Chris enjoys moving mountains."

Rev. Dr. Ted Sauter, Senior Pastor, North Naples United Methodist Church

Reviews for 1-800-For-Women-Only

"It is amazing that a man would want to write about women. That is a change, but Chris has a sense of humor that can make you laugh. Women will enjoy this book and men may gain new insight."

Dorothy K. Ederer, O.P., Director of Campus Ministry,
St. John Student Center, East Lansing, Michigan

"Light, refreshing take on some not so light topics. Wrapped in silliness and wit are serious, social and moral truths that challenge us to be more than ordinary."

Peggy Ryba, Membership Director, North Naples Church, Naples, Florida

"Chris is like a modern day prophet, throwing modern day concepts and concerns out there for us to contemplate. The seeds he tosses can land on sand or soil depending on the reader. I suggest you pull up a nice spot in your garden and sit down and read…then allow some of his thoughts to germinate in your life! "

Mia Guinan, Owner, Gourmet Gang, Camp Trident, Virginia Beach VA

"Paradox is a person that combines contradictory features. Chris Bent is a paradox. Reading his most recent works I am not surprised by the depth, humor, passion and spirituality. In spite of mixed content the flow between chapters allows you to enjoy the paradox. Chris' muses have caused a few smiles; some ponderings and touched my heart. Let this Paradox of a Man walk up to you and continue the conversation.

Nancy Lascheid, RN, BSN, Co-Founder, Neighborhood Health Clinic, Naples, Florida

"1-800-For-Women-Only or the "Mystery of Women" is interesting because it is brutally accurate. In fact, it is frightening to read the explanations of characteristics of women. Many of these things I had not even been aware of, but they are "right on target". The book is written with great sensitivity and insight. I never got the feeling that women were criticized, but accepted as observed. It is an easy fun read and a great gift to give to a friend or even a son who is even thinking of getting married. As the mother of three sons, I know it is true; "Heart-felt is at the core of being. Being somebody."

Sue Lester, Volunteer, Children's Coalition of
Collier County, Pilot Club, Naples, Florida

"Chris Bent's extraordinary life has given him a perspective that so very few have. His insight comes not only from his incredible experiences but from his deeply rooted sense of responsibility, caring, and love for others. His thoughtful mind is not on idle, but instead always on overdrive, crystallizing in well thought out words those concepts that would have many times escaped us, were it not for the efforts of this author to engage, care deeply, and then, as Chris has done so remarkably here, write."

Jennifer L. Whitelaw, Attorney, Whitelaw Legal Group, Naples, FL

Reviews for 1-800-Laughing-Out-Loud

"Chis is a stew: meat, potatoes, veggies, gravy, biscuits and mustard. A warm, tender mix of good taste, generous servings, and something for all appetites! Chris mixes a Hunter S. Thompson "Gonzo Journalism" writing style with a Soupy Sales "Pie in the Face" sense of humor. Chris writes about: Life Values, Family, Self, Respect, Good & Evil. His perspective of life's Value Proposition engages our brain to think about ourselves and others. Chris' previous books are from the Heart and Soul. Take his counsel of his life's experience. There is good advice in each chapter! You will enjoy each word like every bite of a good stew."

Gerry Ross, Executive, Pratt & Whitney (Retired)

"Chris Bent is the type of guy you want to share a cold beer with at the end of a lousy day and have him philosophize on the real meaning of life. Since you might not have that opportunity anytime soon let me suggest you read 1-800-LAUGHING-OUT-LOUD. Perfect title for the book, because when reading it you will."

Nancy Lascheid, RN, BSN, Co-Founder, Neighborhood Health Clinic, Naples, Florida

Reviews for 1-800-Oh-My-Goodness

"With 1-800-Oh-My-Goodness, Chris Bent offers his thoughts on a variety of topics, in order to amuse, inspire, and challenge any reader. With his witty insight, and perspective forged from life experience, Chris seeks to help us all become better individuals."

Michael Hopkins, Attorney, Naples, FL

"In this book Chis is honest and open with the reader. He definitely gives you a lot to ponder. You can't wait to see what he is going to share next."

Dorothy K. Ederer O.P., Director of Campus Ministry, St. John Student Center

"Oh my goodness", Chris has again presented a faith filled and thought provoking book. His stream of thought, that often reads more like poetry than prose, will cause you to rethink moments of life in a context of love and promise."

Rev Jean Moorman Brindel, CFRE, AFP, Associate Director of Development, Emeritus United Theological Seminary, Dayton Ohio

"Honest, incisive, poetic and profound: the writings of Chris Bent. Passion for people, the nation and the world spring from his pages; provocative questions leap from the shortest chapters ever. Silent voices speak in these pages and nothing is to be taken for granted, for life and love run deep between the lines of 1-800- Oh-My-Goodness. "

Wendy J. Deichmann, PhD, President, United Theological Seminary

Reviews for 1-800-For-SEALS-Only

"Pungent, cogent, wistful, idealistic, naive, wise, — all in no particular sequence, reflecting a view of life that it is all unpredictable, and it is mental, physical & moral preparation that will sustain us... there are life lessons and observations here for anyone and everyone...."

Lt (jg) James Hawes, BUDS 29E, SEAL, CIA, (He was the First SEAL In Africa)...(sadly was my UDTR Instructor too)

"Who knew SEALs could write? (LOL) But what Chris does with his gift is really less "writing" than it is expressing the "unwritten." We all have our thoughts; and Frogmen have certain very special and unique shared experiences. Chris puts the pen to the task of relating what we (the Frogs) have experienced and what we (all of his readers) now observe in sharing the experience of the world around us. It's challenging and funny (if you've been through a "real Hell Week"), and sometimes sad. But hey, isn't life? Hooyah!"

Timothy Phillips, SEAL, BUDS 166, ST-8, ST-4

"Chris - great stuff…as always. "Hooyah Mike"…"Every sin is a grenade"…"My wife is my swim buddy"…great thoughts as only a SEAL can put into words. I love it and will BUY a few copies for my Assistant Sergeant at Arms to read to guide their young lives… Hooyah Chris and see you soon!"

Phil King, Sergeant at Arms, NC Senate, BUDS 32

"Mr. Bent's words of wisdom on some of the evolutions of U. S. Navy SEAL training are demonstrated to apply to everyday life with such simplicity. God, Family, Country, is the essence of being an honorable and patriotic American. It is the ethos of the Navy SEAL credo. The band of brothers whose lives are bonded as one in being; all for one and one for all! Nothing in this world feels better to receive in life as the emblem, the SEAL Trident, of a true warrior and to receive into one's heart the holy trinity! Hooyah! The only easy day was yesterday!"

Erasmo Elijah Riojas (Doc Rio) HMC (SEAL) Ret.

"I am a SEAL Teammate of LT. Chris Bent. During our years of serving our country as Naval Special Warfare Operatives, Chris always manifested that "Can Do" attitude so necessary for success in what many would consider: "A tough way to make a living!"

Among other sub-specialties, Chris and I had the honor of being the Platoon Commanders who would "Recover Astronauts!" Within the pages of "1-800-FOR-SEALS-ONLY", you will get to see the mind-set of students going through BUDS Training (still the toughest Military Training in the World) with most Classes experiencing an over 80% Drop Out Rate! Chris masterfully combines our training to current issues existing today. A Giant HOOYAH for a must read publication! 1-800-FOR-SEALS-ONLY is awarded a big BRAVO ZULU from your old Teammates!"

Dr. Frank Cleary, OIC, Seventh Platoon, ST-2 (Ret.)

"One need only look into the night sky to recognize that there is brilliance in chaos. One need only read this book to realize the same. Intertwined in stories, random thoughts, and opinions one will find extraordinary pearls of wisdom in here…and a lot of them. Chris is brilliant."

Navy SEAL Commander

"Dear Frogfather, Your writings remind me of the lessons and examples that were taught to me and my siblings by my parents, grandparents and the nuns that taught me in parochial school. I am so blessed to have them in my life. We are also blessed to have you because you have taken the time and effort to put down in writing your thoughts. They are insightful, and positive, to help us lead a better life. Thank you."

Maureen Murphy, Mother of LT. Michael Murphy,
Medal of Honor recipient, BUD/S Class 236, SDVT-1

"Five Stars for the FROGFATHER! This is a great book, and should be required reading…."

Commander (SEAL) Tom Hawkins, USN, Ret., author, NSW Historian

"Chris Bent has again taken his many and varied life experiences and applied them to life in general and "how to do it right". This book is clearly for everyone, not just SEAL's. Life was never meant to be easy and all of us can take away something from this book and the Frogman saying "The only easy day was yesterday". Even if it is the hard way....do the right thing.

From one Frogman to another I say to Chris, your eulogy (chapter 75) should be read when the time comes: Teammate, seen or unseen, you truly have made a difference!

Hooyah 1-800-For-SEALS-Only!"

Mike Macready, SEAL Team One, BUD/S 49 West Coast

"Chris Bent's latest 1-800 offering certainly gets my SEAL of approval... Using his own unique blend of insight, intellect and inspiration, Chris lifts parallels from the rich history and tradition behind the US Navy SEALs to provide challenging questions and equally thought provoking answers to this experience that we call life. In this social-networking, politically-corrected day and age where common sense, discipline and values seem to have fallen by the wayside, Chris Bent cuts through like a K-Bar to remind us all exactly what is of the utmost importance."

Darren A. Greenwell - NSW Historian, Researcher, Collector

"Chris Bent's latest 1-800 offering certainly gets my SEAL of approval... Using his own unique blend of insight, intellect and inspiration, Chris lifts parallels from the rich history and tradition behind the US Navy SEALs to provide challenging questions and equally thought provoking answers to this experience that we call life. In this social-networking, politically-corrected day and age where common sense, discipline and values seem to have fallen by the wayside, Chris Bent cuts through like a K-Bar to remind us all exactly what is of the utmost importance."

Darren A. Greenwell - NSW Historian, Researcher, Collector

Reviews for 1-800-For-Veterans-Only

"I will always have a special place in my heart for our veterans. Growing up in a military family, I spent my childhood years living on various Air Force bases, learning the lingo, and exploring the far corners of the world while my father flew various missions in both peacetime and conflict. This upbringing has given me a love and appreciation of anything written about the military, whether it be a Tom Clancy thriller or a World War II biography. Author Chris Bent has written some wonderful books in the past few years and I simply love his latest, "1-800-For-Veterans-Only".

Bent definitely has a way with words and his short essays on a variety of topics are conversational, often very witty, and sometimes quite touching. There are so many things that are touched on in this read that it would be impossible not to strike a chord with someone who has had any connection to the military over their lifetime, myself included. From thoughts on enlisting, experiences at boot camp, early days in the service and the uncertainties faced, to the battleground itself. Bent discusses not only what it's like to come home after a deployment, but the experiences of being a veteran and some of the darker aspects of this that we see in our country today.

One of the things that I found most inspiring about Bent's latest was his ability to speak directly to those veterans who may be out there and possibly struggling. There is some very sage wisdom in this one and it certainly has the potential to turn some lives around. Very well done."

TFL READER – Amazon Book Reviewer

A Veteran's Comment on the Chapter "The Hand"

"I agree because when this USMC veteran returned home there were no handshakes or high fives but plenty of shaken fists.

I'm reminded of a verse from "Where No One Stands Alone"

"Hold my hand all the way every hour every day

From here to the great unknown

Take my hand let me stand

Where no one stands alone."

There are two photos of hands representing two distinct eras:

The first is a stained glass window in a Chapel at Paris Island. S.C., with The Hand of God holding 12 Marines from my unit who were killed on Jan. 20, 1968 in Quang Tri Province, Vietnam.

The second is a marble work entitled "Hand in Hand" that stands at the entrance of a children's rehabilitation clinic in Dong Ha, Vietnam, just a few miles from the site where the above Marines were killed."

Floyd Killough, USMC (Ret.)

www.ingramcontent.com/pod-product-compliance
Lightning Source LLC
Chambersburg PA
CBHW071525040426

42452CB00008B/897